Centering Prayer

Centering Prayer in Daily Life and Ministry

Edited by Gustave Reininger

2005

The Continuum International Publishing Group Inc
15 East 26 Street, New York, NY 10010

Printed in the United States of America

Library of Congress Cataloging-in-Publication Data

Centering prayer in daily life and ministry / edited by Gustave Reininger
p. cm.
Includes bibliographical references.
ISBN 0-8264-1041-3
1. Contemplation. 2. Prayer—Christianity. 3. Pastoral theology.
I. Keating, Thomas. II. Reininger, Gustave.
BV5091.C7C4 1997
248.3'2—DC21 97-33168
CIP

Contents

Foreword

GUSTAVE REININGER

The generous support of the Parish of Trinity Church in New York City has made this book possible. The Rev. Daniel Paul Matthews, Trinity's rector, and its vestry had the foresight three years ago to explore a new direction of supporting parish-based programs in Christian spirituality. Trinity recognized that the mainline religions should not only lead but also participate in a renewal of Christian contemplative spirituality. Under the direction of the Rev. James Callaway, Jr., and his colleague, Dr. Robert Carle, the Trinity Grants Program actively searched for established initiatives in parish-based spirituality which needed support.

Among the first spirituality grants was support for the Centering Prayer program at the Parish of St. Matthew in Pacific Palisades, California, which had become a center for Contemplative Outreach, the spiritual network that supports those practicing Centering Prayer. The rector, the Rev. David Walton Miller, had made Centering Prayer an essential element among the parish's diverse and active ministries. He shared a conviction that active ministry has to arise from the contemplative dimension of the gospel, the presence and action of Christ within us, lest the ministry itself become depleting, disillusioning, or self-aggrandizing. Under the direction of Gale Warren Reininger, the St. Matthew's initiative has conducted over forty-five Centering Prayer workshops and retreats in the past five years, teaching Centering Prayer to several thousand participants. In an outreach from St. Matthew's, Centering Prayer programs have been offered in

Folsom Prison, in African-American and Hispanic churches, and in other parishes from Los Angeles to Washington, D.C., from Seattle to Tennessee. We are most grateful to Mr. and Mrs. Terry Inch, whose great support and generosity in 1992 made it possible for the Centering Prayer Program to begin this ministry in the Parish of St. Matthew and so many other churches and parishes.

The common thread that links the contributors to this collection is their participation in the Centering Prayer program at St. Matthew's. For some St. Matthew's provided a first opportunity to teach Centering Prayer without subjecting their home congregations to experimentation. For others, a workshop at St. Matthew's was an opportunity to open new dimensions to their Contemplative Prayer ministries. Indeed, one of the goals of the Trinity grant was to encourage new voices to write on Centering Prayer.

We are also deeply grateful for the support of the Rt. Rev. Frederick Borsch, the bishop of the Episcopal Diocese of Los Angeles, particularly for his encouragement to offer Centering Prayer in the parishes in his diocese. A special appreciation is extended to the Rt. Rev. Robert Andersen, retired bishop of Minnesota and now assistant bishop of Los Angeles, for his devotion to the contemplative dimension of prayer and his constant support and collaboration. Bishop Andersen established, with the generous support of Abbot Jerome Thiesen, OSB, an Episcopal House of Prayer on the grounds of the Roman Catholic Benedictine Abbey of St. John's at Collegeville, Minnesota, which is a thriving prayer center that binds the Anglican and Roman Catholic theological traditions here in America.

This book, with its ecumenical group of contributors, celebrates Centering Prayer as a common ground for Christian unity. It marks the first time that people other than William Meninger, Basil Pennington, and Thomas Keating (the three Trappist monks who distilled Centering Prayer from the Christian contemplative heritage) have written in depth on Centering Prayer, its benefits and effects in daily life and ministry.

Many of its contributors are of the Anglican Communion, giving testament that Contemplative Outreach, the spiritual network dedicated to sharing the gift of Centering Prayer, is diversely formed by the various denominations present in the network and united in a common search for God and the lived experience of Christ through Centering Prayer. Without the vision of Gene Gollogly of The Continuum Publishing Company, this volume would not have been attempted.

As Centering Prayer is adopted by the broader Christian community and as ". . . people grow in grace and experience, various other expressions of the [contemplative] vision may unfold."[1] It is exactly the bold creativity found in this book that Thomas Keating encourages in those who have grown in the contemplative dimension of prayer:

> The very nature of growth in contemplation produces the liberation of creative energies not previously experienced. If we give people a deep contemplative grounding, they will have a better chance of fulfilling whatever ministry to which God may call them.[2]

This volume itself is an expression of deep gratitude for the friendship, encouragement, and constant support Abbot Thomas Keating has extended to all the authors. His ministry of sharing Centering Prayer is the inspiration and motivation for these offerings on how Centering Prayer can enliven daily life and ministry with the living presence of Christ.

---

1. Thomas Keating, foreword to *The Contemplative Outreach Handbook.*
2. Ibid.

Introduction

BASIL PENNINGTON

Centering Prayer — the name has certainly caught on. I can remember well when it first began to be used. It was at the first prayershop we did outside of the monastic retreat house. The program was sponsored by the Conference of Major Superiors of Men and the Religious Leadership Conference of Women. There was a team working with me. I had had the privilege of knowing and working with one of the greatest spiritual fathers of our century, Fr. Louis (Thomas Merton) of Gethsemani. In the course of this initial prayershop I quoted him frequently, using such quotes as: "The best way to come to God is to go to your own center and pass through that center into the center of God." After a number of quotes like that, Fr. Armand Proulx, the provincial of the La Salette Fathers, began to call our "Prayer of the Cloud" Centering Prayer. Our traditional little method came home from the prayershop with a new name.

Today it is used in all parts of our small world. I have had the privilege of sharing it in China and South Africa, in Sri Lanka and England, in Singapore and New York. This year's itineraries include Malaysia, India, Switzerland, France, England, Uganda, Kenya, Brazil, United States, Mexico, and China.

This volume gives witness to something else. This precious part of our heritage, which, like the fire of the Temple, was hidden in the deep well of a few monasteries, is burning brightly again, within all parts of the Christian family. The Contemplative Outreach, frequently mentioned in these articles, is truly an ecumenical movement. Then there is the Mastery Foundation, an interreligious effort to bring the empowerment of this prayer back to Christian communities and to share it with members of the other great world religions who have so generously shared their heritages with Christians.

Last week I had breakfast with one of my publishers. He had published one of my books on Centering Prayer, so he is familiar with it. But he has not practiced it himself. In the course of the breakfast he raised what is often a concern of those who have not had the experience of the prayer in their lives: Isn't there danger that this form of prayer will lead to too individualistic a relationship with God causing one to lose all social concern? We have been proud — Lord, forgive us — of the close relationship of Centering Prayer with Food for the Poor, a powerfully effective outreach to the poorest of the poor in the Caribbean, which has come out of Centering Prayer. The articles in this volume, especially Fr. Thomas Keating's, make it abundantly clear that a proper and faithful practice of Centering Prayer will always lead to a very generous "contemplative service." This is why Mother Teresa of most blessed memory had repeatedly asked me to lead Centering Prayer prayershops not only for her novices but also for her superiors in different parts of the world.

I am grateful to Gus Reininger, who worked so effectively to put this together, and all the contributors to this volume not only for their fine presentations here but for the wonderful, effective work they have each been doing to bring this most precious part of the ancient Christian heritage to their respective Christian churches as well as to the Church as a whole. And I am grateful to Gene Gollogly and the folks at Continuum for providing this opportunity to bring our voices to all you our friends who read and are nourished by these pages. May each one of you not only be personally nourished by these pages but in turn bring this portion of the Good News to your brothers and sisters in your ecclesial community and beyond.

1 ❖

The Practice of Attention / Intention

THOMAS KEATING

The practice of Centering Prayer, built upon *lectio divina,* is based on a millennium of Christian contemplative tradition. The barriers that we have created and our own internal "noise," however, must be overcome before we can fully allow the silence of God to well up from within and heal us. Our spiritual journey, therefore, requires not only a practice like Centering Prayer leading to contemplation, but also practices for daily life such as methods of right attention (to what we are doing) and intention (to why we are doing it).

The teaching of the Divine Indwelling is a fundamental doctrine for the spiritual journey. The Father, the Son as the Eternal Word of the Father, and the Holy Spirit are present within us. These relationships, which are never separate in their unity, are forever interacting. The Father is the potentiality for all existence; the Son is the actuality of all possibilities of existence; and the Spirit is the love that motivates both. Love loving itself eternally in the Trinity is the basis of our own existence, the most intimate part of us, that which is most real in us, the part of us that is capable of infinite happiness through participation in the divine life.

The true self, that which we are trying to awaken through spiritual practice, is not separate from God. The true self is the divine manifesting itself in our uniqueness, in our talents, in our personal history, in our cultural conditioning, and in the rest of the complex factors that go into making up our conscious life and its manifestation in our various activities. In spite of the obstacles we place in opposition to that manifestation, the infinite tenderness of God is present in us right now. Because of what traditional theology calls the fallen human condition, however, we are out of touch with this enormous energy of love that is inviting us to participate.

This does not mean that we have no identity of our own. Nor does it mean total absorption into God, as it does in some Eastern traditions. It does not mean the total loss of self. We remain uniquely whoever we are in virtue of our creation, but there is no possessiveness toward that uniqueness. The movement of the Spirit prompts us to give back whatever we are, all that we are, as much as we are, and everything that we have received from God. To give all back to God in love is the work of everyday life.

Around the true self there is a circle of awareness that we might call our spiritual nature. It has two principal faculties, the passive intellect and the will-to-God. These are, respectively, the innate desire for infinite truth and the innate desire for boundless love. Because of our fallen human condition, we are not normally in touch with our spiritual nature. Unconnected, our actual psychological consciousness on a day-to-day level is a "homemade," false self manifesting itself and not God.

The spiritual journey begins when we become aware that our ordinary psychological consciousness is dominated by the false self with its programs for happiness and overidentification with our cultural conditioning. The spiritual journey involves an inner change of attitude beginning with the recognition of being out of contact with our spiritual nature and our true self, and taking means to return. Only then can our true self and the potentiality that God has given us to live the divine life be manifested. Contemplative service is action coming from the true self, from our inmost being.

To liberate our true self is an
takes time. Centering Prayer is cor
program of liberation. It would be a
Prayer as a mere rest period or a per
sometimes provides these things. Ne
You might find some bliss along the
to endure the wear and tear of the disc
or silence.

Thinking our usual thoughts is th ... nan
nature has devised for us to hide from ... conscious. When our minds begin to quiet down in Centering Prayer, up comes the emotional debris of a lifetime in the form of gradual (and sometimes dramatic) realizations of what the false self is. We also learn how this homemade self that we constructed in early childhood to deal with unbearable pain became misdirected into seeking substitutes for God. Images that do not really have any existence except in our imagination are projected on other people instead of facing head-on their source in ourselves.

Consider the Beatitudes (Matt. 5:3–12). The capacity to practice them are within us as part of our baptism. Similarly, the gifts and fruits of the Spirit enumerated by Paul in Galatians 5 are vibrating within us all the time. They are mediated through the various levels of the psyche so that we do not experience their power until they are awakened through the discipline of deep prayer. Of course, there are other ways that God has of awakening us to the divine. God is, for instance, perfectly free to reach up and pull us down into that area at any time, but we should not count on it. It is *better* to practice a discipline.

What would be an active discipline to assist our Centering Prayer, so that it does not become self-centered or a mere process of self-perfection, so that it actually is the assimilation of the infinite tenderness of God living within us? In general, such a discipline might be called "contemplative service." I call it the "attention/intention practice."

When we emerge from Centering Prayer, the present moment is what we confront when we open our eyes. We have been in the present moment of prayer when we were completely vine life and action within us. Then we get out of nd continue daily life. This is where attentiveness to tent of the present moment is a way of putting order into myriad occupations, thoughts, and events of daily life. Attention to this context simply means to do what we are doing. This was one of the principal recommendations of the Desert Fathers and Mothers of the fourth century. The disciple would come for instruction and say, "I am interested in finding the true self and becoming a contemplative. What should I do?" The desert guides would reply in the most prosaic language, "Do what you're doing," which means, bring your attention to the present moment and its immediate context and keep it there. For instance, it is time for supper. Well, put the food on the table. This is true virtue. Turning on the television at that time or making a needless phone call might not be. Attending to the present moment means that our mind is on what we are doing as we go through the day. We are thus united to God in the present moment instead of wondering about what we are going to do next or tomorrow. There might be an appropriate time to set aside for planning but not now.

To be completely present to someone with whom you are talking is one of the most difficult of all practices. Your presence will often do more than what you say. It gives others a chance to be present to themselves. Moreover, if your presence is coming from a deep place within, the divine compassion that is inspiring you will be there for them in the degree that they are capable of receiving it.

To be totally present to children if you have them, to the elderly if you have them, to counselees if you have them, to the job of the present moment that needs a responsible fulfillment—this is what might be called how to act from the center, how to do contemplative service, how to put order into ordinary daily life by being present to the occupation of the present moment. This cuts off an enormous amount of needless reflection, projects of self-aggrandizement, and wondering what people are thinking of us.

If we refuse to think of anything except what we are doing or the person that we are with, we develop the habit of being present to the present moment. In a way, the present moment becomes as sacred as being in church. Far better to be present to your duty if you are a bartender than to be present in church and thinking about being in a bar. At least you are present to yourself when you are paying attention to what you are doing.

Attention, then, is a way of doing what we are doing. It cracks the crust of the false self (our psychological awareness of daily life) in which we are the center of the universe while everything else is circling around our particular needs or desires. The false self is an illusion, but unfortunately it is a heritage we all bring with us from early life.

A practice, then, of paying attention just to what we are doing for a certain part of the day for the love of God, disregarding every other thought, is a practical way of opening ourselves to a deeper level of contemplation. It will not work instantly, but regular practice has long-range effects. It might be called the *how* of activity.

The spiritual level is also healed of the false self by the why of what we are doing. Our intention to do what we are doing for the love of God powerfully connects us with the divine presence. The power of intention is immense. The will willing God actually enters into union with God although we may not consciously experience the effects of the union right away. My intention is why I am doing what I am doing.

Here is the practice: We choose a certain time to establish and renew our intention of doing some particular work for the love of God. Our minds are generally so scattered that we often forget. To have a set time or particular activity when we do this deliberately as a daily practice will quickly demonstrate the influence of intentionality on the false self. Nobody does anything without a motive. We do not know why we are doing something unless we know both our conscious and unconscious motivation. For example, as soon as we start trying to do a particular job for the love of God, the motivation of the false self begins to arise: we may find ourselves acting out of jealousy, we may want to get even with someone who has wronged us, or we might try to get ahead in some situation and trample on someone else's rights.

The galaxy of bad intentions motivated by the false self emerges even when we try to maintain a pure intention for a few minutes.

The great insight of the early Desert Fathers and Mothers was that a pure intention leads to purity of heart; selfish motivation is gradually eliminated and the habit of a pure intention is firmly established. We begin to enter into God's intentionality, which is to manifest infinite compassion in the present circumstances, however painful, however joyful, however seemingly bereft of the divine presence.

As soon as we focus our intention—*why* we are doing this particular action—our unconscious motivation arises. The unconscious motivation might be that in our service, however devoutly it may appear to others, what we are really seeking is praise. In other words, our secret desires begin to emerge into our consciousness when we deliberately focus our intention on loving God in all that we do.

How we work—attention. *Why* we work—intention. This leads to the third and final quality of contemplative service: *Who* is doing the work? Having uncovered the spiritual obstacles of pride, envy, and whatever else might be hidden in the unconscious, we are now approaching our true self. We are approaching our inmost center. We are approaching "Love loving itself." What is going to happen? Without *intending* anything special, without necessarily *doing* anything special, people begin to find God in us as we humbly do what we are supposed to be doing. Complete submission to God allows the divine energy to radiate, and others seeing this have a sense of being in touch with God or in the midst of a community where divine love exists. This is what a Christian community is supposed to be, whether it is a family, parish, or organization. This third way of working or acting in daily life might be called "transmission."

When attention to the present moment and a pure intention are established as habits, then we have, in the fullest sense of the word, contemplative service. Our contemplation is thus perceived, enjoyed, and received, perhaps without a word being spoken, or without anyone being able to explain it. People know that, somehow, Christ is active and present in us—and loving *them* through us. This is the atmosphere in which people can grow and become fully alive. One needs to feel loved as a human being to come alive. The greatest love, of course, is divine love, especially when it becomes transparent in others. And divine love is most impressive when such persons are not even aware of it, when that love just happens.

2 ❁

Lectio Divina: The Gate Way to the Spiritual Journey and Centering Prayer

BASIL PENNINGTON

During the past couple of years, from places as diverse as Manila and Manchester, I have received requests from leaders in the Centering Prayer movement to conduct programs about *lectio divina* or, more simply, *lectio*. It seems to me that *lectio* is a Latin word that has now come into its own in the English language. Simple translation—"reading"—too completely betrays the richness of the centuries-old tradition that this little word carries.

We did, indeed, in the very first prayershops we presented and in the first books I published, *Daily We Touch Him* and *Centering Prayer,* include practical teaching in regard to *lectio*. We never lost sight of the fact that *lectio* provides the traditional context for Centering Prayer. But in those early days, participants were so keenly interested in getting in touch with "Christian meditation" that they gave little attention to *lectio*. I think it is a sign of the maturation of the movement that today many who have been practicing Centering Prayer for years are showing a keen interest in *lectio divina.* In the course of this volume you will find it mentioned in every contribution and in some cases it is given a good bit of attention.

The way of *lectio,* coming to its fullness in Centering Prayer, is a call to intimacy with God, a call addressed to everyone. Often the inspired Scriptures couch this call in the symbolism of the nuptials. As we seek to speak about it, perhaps the traditional wedding advice is not out of place: "Something old, something new, something borrowed, something blue." The old is the practice itself, the new is the packaging with various insights. Borrowed was the realization we recieved from our Eastern counterparts of the importance of a simple, practical presentation so that practitioners can easily embark upon the discipline. We need a simple, practical, point-by-point method for *lectio.* I would like to offer that here, going on to underline some of the important elements that support or bring about true *lectio.*

Whether one uses Thomas Keating's more developed, carefully nuanced four-point presentation or our earlier three-point one, it is clear that the essence of *lectio* is presupposed. We cannot "consent to God's presence and action within," if we do not know God and know that God is present. We cannot love God "who dwells in the center of our being" if we do not know this God and know he is here. We cannot love one whom we do not know. For the Christian, faith is the key here. And faith comes through hearing. And *lectio* is precisely this: hearing the Word of God speaking to us in and through his inspired Word.

Here are the guidelines we have usually set forth in the course of our prayershops and writings:

THE METHOD OF LECTIO

It is well to keep the Sacred Scriptures enthroned in our home in a place of honor as a Real Presence of the Word in our midst.

1. Take the Sacred Text with reverence and call upon Holy Spirit.

2. For ten minutes (or longer, if you are so drawn) listen to the Lord speaking to you through the Text, and respond.

3. At the end of the time, choose a word or phrase (perhaps one will have been "given" to you) to take with you, and thank the Lord for being with you and speaking to you.

More briefly we might put it this way:

1. Come into the Presence and call upon Holy Spirit.
2. Listen for ten minutes.
3. Thank the Lord and take a "word."

We Christians, along with our brothers and sisters in the Jewish faith, believe in the book we call the Bible. We believe that the authors and editors that brought this collection into being were especially guided by Holy Spirit to include in this writing only those things and all those things that God wanted written for our instruction. We believe that this grace-laden activity leads to a special abiding presence of God in his Word. In our respective liturgies we proclaim this in many ways.

If *lectio* engenders faith, it nonetheless must itself be approached in faith. It is precisely our belief, set forth so powerfully in the Dogmatic Constitution on Revelation of the Second Vatican Council, that God is truly present in the inspired Word that makes *lectio* different from simple "reading." *Lectio* is an actual experiential meeting with God in and through the inspired Word. And it is Holy Spirit, who inspired these texts and who dwells in us to teach us all things, bringing to mind all that Jesus taught us, on whom we depend to bring this experience about.

Because God is present, speaking to us, it is not reading; it is listening to God speaking to us. *Lectio* needs the leisure of a friendly conversation. So we do not pace it by a page, paragraph, or chapter that has to be got through. Rather we give it some quality time and just be with our Friend. God's first word might be enough to fill the whole of the time we can allow for our get-together. Or God might take quite a few words. When God speaks we respond.

When I share this method of *lectio* with a group, after we have gone over the three steps, I invite them to actually spend a few minutes in *lectio*. At the end of that time, I invite them to share with their neighbor their "experience of God during the reading." At the end of the sharing I then ask them: Did you share with your neighbor some of the insights and ideas that came to you during the *lectio* or did you, as I asked, share with your neigbor your experience of God during the *lectio?* After a couple moments of silence there is usually an "Ohhhh." We go to *lectio* not to get insights and ideas—although we usually do get some of these—but we go to *lectio* to experience God; to come to know God—by being with God—and not just know about God. We depend on Holy Spirit acting through the gifts of the Spirit to bring us to this experience.

At the end of the time, we thank the Lord. Again this is emphasizing the reality of the presence. Almighty God has deigned to sit down and talk with us. Thanks is certainly in order.

And we do not want to go away from the meeting empty-handed. Sometimes God will have given us a "word"—some word, sentence, or phrase that has really spoken to us and which will perhaps remain with us for the rest of our lives. Sometimes, though, it will seem as though we have just heard words, words, words. And none of them have really spoken to us. Then we will have to pull out something from the text ourselves. In any case we take a "word of the Lord" with us. And this is the beginning of *meditatio.*

We keep the Latin word *lectio* because the simple translation "reading" would in no wise convey the richness of this personal encounter with God. We also keep it because in the tradition *lectio* bespoke a whole way of walking with the Lord, summed up in the four words: *lectio, meditatio, oratio,* and *contemplatio.*

Even in Guigo the Carthusian, writing in the late twelfth century, the influence of the emerging scholasticism and its rationalizing effect on the spiritual journey is in evidence as meditation is presented more as a thinking over what had been received in *lectio.* This was not the way of the many previous centuries. Rather than seeking to fit the received word into the very limited parameters of our human concepts and ideas, the earlier practice allowed the word by its presence to expand the parameters of the mind so that the meditator began to see things more God's way.

Some of the contributions in this book reflect the more modern, rationalistic approach to meditation rather than the earlier, receptive mode, which in fact better disposed the recipient to move on to the openness and receptivity of contemplation. While this earlier method of meditation can easily enough lead into the conversation of prayer, it can more easily open out into silent communications of love.

Maybe here I could bring in that "something blue"—for that color calls to the mind of many the holy Virgin Mary, a true model and patron for those who center. Luke tells us that Mary "pondered all these things in her heart." She didn't try to think them over or reason them out. She rather allowed the magnitude of the events and the revelation given her to rest in her until they expanded her consciousness so that she could live a total consent to God's presence and action within her.

Let us just look at this for a moment. Here was this very young Jewish girl, totally formed by the Jewish ethos. For her there was one God and he was the God of her people. This was their hope and their glory. Suddenly a heavenly messenger reveals to her not only that this God has a Son but that this God wants her to be the mother of that Son. We have here in essence the two central mysteries of the Christian faith: the Trinity and the Incarnation. Mary allowed this revelation to expand her consciousness until she was able to give a fully human, graced consent to this action of the God present within her. This is precisely what we want to do with the word of revelation that we receive in our *lectio*. This is the traditional understanding of *meditatio*.

All four elements—*lectio, meditatio, oratio* and *contemplatio:* receiving the Word, letting it work in us, responding, and resting in love—can be present in any period of *lectio,* if we but give the Spirit time and freedom to act within us. This is the gracious gift of God, for we do not know how to pray as we ought. It is not always given. And any particular period of *lectio* may not get beyond the simple *lectio* stage. So we go forth with our chosen "word," opening ourselves, allowing this fourfold way to be embrace the whole of our day.

As we walk through the day's activities with our chosen or received "word," the Word walks with us, through the word, enabling us to see more fully how God sees things and the events of the day. Prayer is our spontaneous response to this enlightening and consoling and strengthening presence. And if we are wise, the time comes twice a day for us to let everything else rest in the secure hands of Divine Providence for a few minutes while we rest in the embrace of his all-caring love.

The spiritual journey then begins with listening, hearing the invitation, and letting it have the space in us that it needs to call forth from us a total, transforming response. The Centering Prayer method actually includes the four elements of *lectio.* We move to our sitting because we here and now hear the invitation as it has been engraved in our memories. For a moment it is again a living word that evokes that consent to God's presence and action in us that is the love that allows us to rest in the embrace of Divine Love.

In August of 1997 there was a most extraordinary gathering at the Abbey of Gethsemani in Kentucky. Masters of many Buddhist traditions, including the Dalai Lama, sat down for four days with spiritual fathers and mothers of the Christian traditions to mutually share their experience of spiritual practice. I was struck by the fact that when this encounter was reported in *The Snow Lion,* a Buddhist publication, the Buddhist monk who wrote the report gave the most space to and indeed quoted at length Sr. Margaret Funk's presentation on *lectio divina.* There was an intuitive sense here that lectio is fundamental in the Christian way.

Lectio divina is the gateway to the spiritual journey and to that particular spiritual practice which we today call Centering Prayer.

3 ❈

The Christian Contemplative Tradition and Centering Prayer

GUSTAVE REININGER

Justifiably, much has been made of the unique contribution to contemporary spirituality by the three Trappist monks who distilled Centering Prayer from the Christian contemplative tradition. William Meninger's instinct to draw on the simple prayer method in *The Cloud of Unknowing,* from which the basic elements of Centering Prayer are distilled, is a model of recovering in a contemporary context a classic of mystical theology. Basil Pennington's book, *Centering Prayer,*[1] was the first complete writing on the practice of Centering Prayer, providing the first exposure of this prayer practice beyond the retreat guest houses at St. Joseph's Abbey in Spencer, Massachusetts, where it quietly evolved in the 1970s. Thomas Keating refined the practice and developed a conceptual background to the prayer and its effects upon daily life.

---

1. M. Basil Pennington, *Centering Prayer: Renewing an Ancient Christian Prayer Form* (New York: Image Books, 1980).

What distinguishes Keating's work from his fellow originators is the context in which it arose, that is, the unfolding experiences of a consciously elected network of persons and small faith communities committed to a regular practice of Centering Prayer. Indeed, one of the most distinguishing characteristics of the Centering Prayer movement is Contemplative Outreach, an ecumenical network founded in 1984 to support those practicing Centering Prayer.[2] It is the corporate experience of this primarily lay movement over the past fifteen years that has provided Keating with not only practical inspiration but also verification of his insights into the contemplative dimension of the spiritual journey. Through Contemplative Outreach workshops, seminars, and retreats, Keating has been able to hear constant reports of the deepening of prayer in the lives of active people. These prayer experiences were often expressed as practitioners' needs to understand the moments of Centering Prayer and to see how it relatesto the tenets and traditions of Christianity. Keating's work as such is not merely theoretical or scholarly but practical—meant both as a *vade mecum,* a "how to" approach to contemplative prayer, and a "what happens" with a regular practice, which is the contemplative dimension of the spiritual journey.

Keating also draws heavily on his fifty years of formation as a Cistercian monk: formal theological training, four years as novice master, and twenty-three years as abbot. Most importantly, he is a committed contemplative who practices what he preaches.

Centering Prayer itself is hardly the first time spiritual practices from the monastic milieu have been distilled for an immediate experience of God *without* theological reflection. *The Imitation of Christ,*[3] the central practice of the fourteenth-century lay movement *Devotio Moderna,* based on *lectio divina,* fostered interior

---

2. Contemplative Outreach was founded in May 1984 as an ecumenical movement that initially included Roman Catholics, Episcopalians, and Methodists.

3. Traditionally ascribed to Thomas à Kempis. See William C. Creasy, *The Imitation of Christ* (Macon, Ga.: Mercer University Press, 1989). Cf. Richard P. McBrien, *Catholicism* (Minneapolis: Winston Press, 1981), 1.1065.

purification through allegorical identification with the life of Christ. With its beginnings in the Low Countries as the Brethren of the Common Life, *Devotio Moderna* spread throughout western Europe providing impetus for ecclesiastical reform, seeking "to use the moral powers issuing from prayer as a means of self-discipline."[4] Reformation spirituality continued this tradition, insisting that "access to God is direct and unmediated, guided by the interior illumination of the Holy Spirit."[5] The Catholic Reformation found a methodology, Ignatian exercises (also based in *lectio divina),* for adherents in active ministry and lay life, which emphasized direct experience and "insisted on the fundamental connection between prayer and the apostolate."[6]

Despite such notable precedents, Centering Prayer still tends to be viewed as a unique, new, or nontraditional practice. Perhaps this point of view is exacerbated because the Christian tradition of integrated contemplative spirituality is "now severely attenuated or even broken—not only in our Western society at large but in the very Church of God—it takes a conscious, and at times heroic, effort to become reconnected to a life-giving tradition."[7] In fostering a reconnection, Keating's contributions have often been hyperbolized as unique discoveries of the contemplative dimension, ranging from a Christian analogue of the alchemist's stone to spiritual substances of catalytic importance. The tendency to elevate Keating to guru status is quickly and clearly denounced by Keating, who has labored to place himself in the mainstream of Judeo-Christian contemplative tradition.

In order to locate Centering Prayer within the Christian contemplative tradition, it might be helpful to consider some of the principal concepts underlying Centering Prayer as it has evolved to date. This is not intended to be a scholarly analysis or an apologia of

---

4. Thomas Keating, *Finding Grace at the Center* (Petersham, Mass.: St. Bede Publications, 1978), 38.

5. McBrien, *Catholicism,* 1.1095.

6. Ibid.

7. Diogenes Allen, *Spiritual Awakenings,* Trinity Church Grants Program Annual Report, New York, 1995, 4.

Keating's work. Instead, it hopes to provide reference to antecedents in the Christian tradition to Centering Prayer and its conceptual background, both the practical and theological underpinnings. In the end, however, Centering Prayer is a personal prayer practice and may redefine our contemporary standards of rationality.

Participating in the Trinitarian Relationship

CENTRAL TO KEATING'S spiritual anthropology is one of the most provocative concepts of faith in the Christian tradition: the Divine Indwelling.

> The fundamental goodness of human nature, like the mystery of the Trinity, Grace, and the Incarnation, is an essential element of Christian faith. This basic core of goodness is capable of unlimited development, indeed, of becoming transformed into Christ and deified.[8]

Throughout his work Keating refers to this "fundamental goodness" as the "true self," whose "center of gravity is God." This is in contrast to the "false self," whose "center of gravity is itself," being constituted of a "constellation of pre-rational reactions" reinforced "by all the self-serving habits that have been woven into our personality" since we were born, traditionally known as "the consequences of original sin."[9] Though one of Keating's great pedagogical strengths is his reliance upon contemporary psychology as a means of approaching theology, his concept of human nature—as good but also capable of transformation in Christ and deification—is well grounded in Christian contemplative tradition, reaching from Judaic spirituality through Jesus to contemporary contemplative writers such as Thomas Merton, Pennington, and himself.[10] It is this Christian contemplative tradition that Keating sees as a source of Centering Prayer, a common ground of Christian unity.

---

8. Thomas Keating, *Open Mind, Open Heart* (Amity, N.Y.: Amity House, 1986), 127.

9. Ibid.

10. For a full treatment of Keating's concept, see "The Christian Contemplative Tradition," *Intimacy with God* (New York: Crossroad, 1995), 44.

The Cappadocian Fathers emphasized *theosis* (deification) as the goal of Christian ascesis. For Origen the soul is "deified by that which it contemplates."[11] Iraneus writes of "a participation *[metoche]* in God."[12] "If the word is made man, it is that men might become gods."[13] For Athanasius, and later for Cyril of Alexandria, it is the "vision of God" through contemplation that purifies and deifies.[14] Gregory of Nyssa claims that "God has made us not simply spectators of the power of God, but also participants in his very nature."[15] His commentary on The Canticle of Canticles sees the soul as the "place of vision" where God dwells in presence, shining in the soul as a mirror. In the Eastern church this concept of deification spread from the desert to become a central doctrine of faith. It "is not some fringe sectarian belief; it is absolutely central to Orthodox theology and to all Orthodox spirituality."[16]

Building on this, the Fathers and Mothers of the Desert emphasized the *imago Dei* as a personal experience of participation in the Trinity: "That man is the image of God who is capable of receiving the knowledge of the Blessed Trinity."[17] Evagrius Ponticus, the first important writer among the Desert Fathers, took the *imago Dei* a step beyond his mentor Gregory of Nyssa. The soul for Evagrius was not merely the mirror of God but the very dwelling place of God's presence. "The image of God . . . is he who has become capable of the unity."[18] John Bamberger notes:

> This unity, as we know, is Evagrius' way of saying that the soul has attained to the perfect knowledge of the Blessed Trinity in loving union. . . . Consequently, for Evagrius, the very definition of man must be established in terms of his contemplation. It is

---

11. Origen, *In Joannem: Sources Chretien,* 32.17.
12. Iraneus, *Adversus Haereses,* 3.20.5.
13. Ibid.
14. Athanasius, *De Incarnationem,* chapter 54..
15. Gregory of Nyssa, *Patriologia Graeca,* 44:1137b.
16. Kenneth Leech, *Soul Friend: An Invitation to Spiritual Direction* (London Sheldon Press, 1977), 143.
17. *Patriologia Graeca,* 3:32.
18. Ibid.

> contemplative union with God which is man's ultimate end, and which establishes man in his full self-realization as the image of God. In this outlook man is not defined as a rational animal (Aristotle) but rather as a being created to be united with God in loving knowledge.[19]

John Çassian, a student and follower of Evagrius, translated the divine union of the Greek fathers for the Latin church even as he helped bring the desert spirituality to the Western church. Divine union remained at the heart of monastic spirituality and was popularized in the sixth century among the laity by the writings of Gregory the Great. It was renewed and fully articulated in the twelfth century by monastic reformers Bernard of Clairvaux and William de Thierry, leaders of the Cistercian revival. With the recovery of "Mystical Theology," a manual on contemplative prayer by Pseudo-Dionysius, the fourteenth-century Rhenish mystics Meister Eckhart, Johannes Tauler, and Jan van Ruysbroeck—contributed to a contemplative renewal, furthering the evolution of experiences of divine union. The fourteenth-century English mystics—the author of *The Cloud of Unknowing*, Walter Hilton, and Julian of Norwich—emphasized practices leading to divine union. In the sixteenth century the Spanish mystics—Theresa of Ávila and John of the Cross—authored towering advancements in the theology of divine union based in praxis.[20]

However enlightened the Christian contemplative tradition, Keating sees this lineage resting on even more fundamental ground: Jesus's explications of divine union and intimacy. Jesus's constant reference to God not as *Elohim* and *El Shaddai,* the god of power and might, the "superhuman world of being and power superior to man,"[21] nor even as *Adonai* and *Yaweh,* the "I am who am"—but as *Abba* signals a distinct shift toward

---

19. Evagrius Ponticus, *The Praktikos Chapters on Prayer,* trans. John Eudes Bamberger, (Spencer, Mass.: Cistercian Publications, 1970), xci–xcii.

20. For a complete treatment of the theology of divine union, see Bernard McGinn, *The Presence of God: A History of Western Christian Mysticism,* vol.1: *The Foundations of Mysticism* (New York: Crossroad, 1991).

21. John L. McKenzie, *Dictionary of the Bible* (New York: Macmillan, 1965), 316.

a new intimacy and relationship with God. *Abba* is the Aramaic address used by children to refer to their father. For Jesus *Abba* "in this context encompasses every human relationship that is beautiful, good, and true, but it especially evokes the sense of parenting, of 'sourcing.'" This, of course, is Jesus's description of the Divine Indwelling, "the most important of all the principles of the spiritual life. It means that *God's own life* is being communicated to us."[22]

Keating sees the very inspiration for Centering Prayer found most distinctly in the final discourse of John where "union language characterizes the Johannine texts as no other early Christian document."[23] Here Jesus offers a report of his very state of consciousness in divine union. "I am in the Father and the Father is in me" (John 14:10). In this final talk with his disciples, in this new dimension of God as *Abba,* Jesus introduces the Trinitarian dimension with mention of the Spirit: "I have said these things to you while I am still with you. But the Advocate, the Holy Spirit, whom the Father will send in my name, will teach you everything, and remind you of all that I have said to you" (John 14:25–26). Jesus invites his disciples to share and live this relationship:

> That they may all be one. As you, Father, are in me and I am in you, may they also be one in us, so that the world may believe that you have sent me . . . so that they may be one, as we are one, I in them and you in me, that they may become completely one. (John 17:21–23a)

The entire goal of the spiritual journey for Keating is to "be in"—and participate in—the life of the Trinitarian relationship. As always, for Keating the question is one of praxis, of personal and direct experience: "As we sit in Centering Prayer, we are connecting with the divine life within us. . . . It is already there waiting to be activated."[24]

As much as Keating sees Centering Prayer as Trinitarian in origin, he also considers it Christological in focus. Centering

22. Keating, *Intimacy with God,* 148.
23. McGinn, *The Presence of God,* 1.78.
24. Keating, *Intimacy with God,* 33.

Prayer is not merely a direct communion of soul with God, either mirroring or presence, defined either as *Abba* or otherwise. The union is accomplished *through* Christ. "As we sit in the presence of the Trinity within us, our prayer unfolds in relationship with Christ." This is not a theological concept but an "existential relationship with Christ as our way into the depths of the Trinitarian relationship." Sitting in Centering Prayer, one is not approaching Christ as "other" but as brother: "Not just juxtaposed to Christ. The movement inward to the Divine Indwelling suggests that our relationship with Christ is an interior one, especially through his Holy Spirit who dwells in us and pours the love of God into our hearts." Because this movement is an experience without theological reflection, "we are relating to the mystery of Christ's passion, death, and resurrection, not as something outside of us but as something inside of us."[25]

It is precisely because Keating insists on divine union not as a concept but as a direct experience that he seems hardly worried about whether the Johannine version of the Divine Indwelling is historically accurate. However, Bernard McGinn, author of the exhaustive four-volume study *The Presence of God*, finds in the text a critical underpinning:

> This union, of course, is resolutely christological. Given the style of this Gospel, in which long discourses placed in Jesus' mouth explain the deeper, hidden meaning of signs, events, and rituals, the "in Christ" formula of Paul is replaced by the phrase *en emoi* ("in me"), frequently used in conjunction with the verb *menein* ("remaining, dwelling"). What is particularly striking about John's use is the mutuality of relations he underscores on all levels of union.[26]

For Keating the distinction is less relevant than his belief that divine union is a living reality of faith that consistently reasserts itself regardless of "time" as the central unifying experience of the Christian contemplative tradition.

---

25. Ibid., 33–34.
26. McGinn, *The Presence of God,* 1.78.

The Fall: The Human Condition

As much as Keating embraces the tradition of divine union, he holds in equal measure (and in seeming contradiction) man's alienation from God as a result of the Fall, or original sin. In an age where many who teach prayer devoid of suffering and sacrifice, as self-affirmation and self-esteem, Keating refuses to blur psychological "feel good" doctrines with fundamental theology. In fact, he stands firm in his conviction of our spiritual impoverishment, of the existential nature of our depravity.

Keating believes "the human race, as a whole, is a sick species," agreeing with Ann Wilson Shaef that up to 96 percent of the population suffer from what she calls "the Addictive Process." Keating connects her psychological diagnosis to the theological doctrine of "original sin."[27]

> If one accepts the traditional doctrine of the consequences of original sin, the freedom to manage one's life is severely limited. It is on the basis of complete helplessness apart from the grace of God that the whole idea of redemption rests.[28]

Keating echoes Augustine's tenet that "the consequences of original sin according to traditional theology are three: illusion, concupiscence, and weakness of will."[29] With these theological concepts firmly fixed, Keating turns to contemporary psychology for an articulation. Indeed, these consequences of original sin manifest themselves as a "false self," which is constituted of our prerational reactions:

> All the self-serving habits [and] emotional damage that [have] come from our early environment and upbringing; all the harm that other people have done to us knowingly or unknowingly at an age when we could not defend ourselves; and the methods we acquired—many of them now unconscious—to ward off the pain of unbearable situations.[30]

---

27. Keating, *Intimacy with God,* 72–73.
28. Ibid., 74.
29. Ibid., 73
30. Keating, *Open Mind, Open Heart,* 128.

A human being coming into individuation or full reflective self-consciousness—with ego intact but *without* the experience of union with God—exhibits patterns of behavior that Keating calls "emotional programs for happiness." Original sin and personal sin have so removed us from our true self that we suffer from "illusion": "Although we are irresistibly programmed for boundless happiness in a way that is inherent to human nature, we do not know where true happiness is to be found."[31]

These "emotional programs for happiness" manifest themselves in human behavior as compulsions and addictions to otherwise healthy instinctual needs of security, power, control, affection, and esteem.[32] We feed these addictions not seeking spiritual fulfillment but pursuing symbols, such as material possessions, manipulation and oppression, and an unweaned need to be popular, loved, and the center of attention (if not the center of the universe). "Concupiscence means that we seek happiness in the wrong places or too much happiness in the right places."[33] These appetites that feed themselves with temporary gratification only reveal an existential void, a nausea. Keating notes that "unfortunately, the average practicing Christian, because of a certain modicum of respectability, does not seem to know this. . . . The practical question for all of us is 'How addicted are we?'"[34]

Eventually, the pursuit of spiritual satisfaction through symbols leads to a psychic and spiritual breakdown, a crisis of faith. This realization by itself, though, is hardly a solution. "If we ever reach the point of finding out where true happiness is to be found, our will is too weak to pursue it."[35] Paul's words remain the state of the art in lamentations about the false self: "I do not do the good I want, but the evil I do not want is what I do. . . . [W]hen I want to do what is good, evil lies close at hand" (Rom. 7:19–21).

---

31. Ibid., 128.

32. Indeed, this is a theological reworking of Abraham Maslow's hierarchy of needs; see, as one example, his *Motivation and Personality* (New York: Harper & Row, 1970).

33. Keating, *Intimacy with God*, 73.

34. Ibid.

35. Ibid.

Keating views the "heart of Christian ascesis [as] the struggle with our unconscious motivations."[36] If one does not become aware of these emotional programs for happiness and confront them in a variety of ways,

> the false self will adjust to any new situation in a short time and nothing is really changed. If we enter the service of the Church, the symbols of security, success, and power in the new milieu will soon become the new objects of our desires. . . . The false self accompanies us, implacably, into whatever lifestyle we choose.[37]

Keating paints a somewhat desperate portrait of the human condition that might place him rather comfortably in the ranks of twentieth-century French existential philosophers or sixteenth-century reformers.

The Journey to Union: Lectio Divina and Centering Prayer

KEATING, OF COURSE, sees conversion as God's response to our awareness of alienation and our dependence on God's mercy. Baptism is the sacrament in which "the false self is ritually put to death."38 One's spiritual journey should continue this execution or crucifixion of the false self that began through the grace of baptism to escape the consequences of sin.

Our willingness to consent to the presence and action of God within us is the hallmark of the contemplative dimension of the spiritual journey. This experience of God's presence is contemplative prayer in its purest form:

> At the still point of the turning world . . .
> I can only say, *there* we have been: but I cannot say where.
> And I cannot say, how long, for that is to place it in time.
> The inner freedom from the practical desire,
> The release from action and suffering, release from the inner

---

36. Thomas Keating, *Invitation to Love: The Way of Christian Contemplation* (Rockport, Mass: Element, 1992), 12.

37. Ibid.

38. Keating, *Open Mind, Open Heart*, 128.

And the outer compulsion, yet surrounded
By a grace of sense, a white light still and moving.[39]

Just how does one experience this still point where our soul meets eternity? For Keating it is God given, but the faculties can be prepared to receive it through the dynamic process of scriptural prayer *(lectio divina)*: the reading of the scriptures *(lectio)*, reflecting *(meditatio)*, responding *(oratio)*, and then resting in God *(contemplatio)*. The goal of *lectio divina*, "resting in God," is described by Evagrius:

> Happy is the spirit that attains to perfect formlessness at the time of prayer . . . that becomes free of all matter and is stripped of all at the time of prayer . . . that attains to complete unconsciousness of all sensible experience at the time of prayer.[40]

Keating with his monastic orientation originally conceived of this process as scripturally based. In the 1970s he and his fellow monks, expecting a deepening of spirituality thanks to Vatican II and a renewal in other denominations, were instead confronted with an exodus of young Christians to Eastern religions for meditation practices. Urging his monks to investigate the wave of spirituality that had hit America and Europe, Keating invited Buddhist masters and teachers of transcendental meditation to the monastery. They soon noticed the ease with which Eastern methods could provide an apophatic experience, which seemed to explain its accessibility and popularity.

Aware that a daily practice of *lectio divina* requires considerable time and the scriptural environment of a monastery, Keating realized that what was good for a monk was not necessarily applicable to people in an active life. He became convinced that some method of prayer from the Christian tradition would be necessary for contemporary people in the active life to reach the contemplative dimension before turning to the fuller practice of *lectio divina*. At this point in the mid-1970s Keating asked his

---

39. T. S. Eliot, *The Complete Poems and Plays* (New York Harcourt, Brace and Co. 1952), 119.

40. Evagrius, *Praktikos*, 75.

chapter to consider how to put the Christian contemplative tradition in a form accessible to active people. He hoped especially to offer an alternative for young Christians practicing Eastern methods who "might be inspired to return to their Christian roots if they knew there was something similar in the Christian tradition."[41]

William Meninger took up the challenge and began investigating ancient Christian methods of prayer. Among others, Meninger explored the method recorded by fourth-century theologian John Cassian in his "Conference Ten": Desert Father Abba Isaac instructed Cassian in a prayer formula, which he claimed had been used by some of the first Desert Fathers and handed down judiciously. The method was to take a phrase from Psalms, "Come to my help, O God; Lord, hurry to my rescue" (cf. 70:2) and to "turn it in a salutary way over and over in your spirit" to "lift yourself upward to the most sublime sights."[42] Abba Isaac recommended praying this formula unceasingly, and in doing so the Fathers probably did not recognize the need for a method practicable for the active life.

Meninger also turned to Pseudo-Dionysius, the sixth-century writer. His method began by reciting the divine names and ended in the highest contemplation of created things, the "way of cataphatic theology" (*Theoria Physike*). Pseudo-Dionysius, however, found this approach limited by its reliance on language and concepts. He then moved to a negative approach, an active denying of all that God is *not*, concluding that "the supreme Cause of every conceptual thing is not itself conceptual." At this point one finds oneself "speechless and unknowing" and at that moment "at one" with the indescribable.[43] This is the apophatic way, the *Theoria Mystike*, the full practice of which probably also requires the time and rhythms of a monastic life.

---

41. Keating, *Intimacy with God,* 15

42. Colm Luibheid, *John Cassian: Conferences* (New York: Paulist, 1985), 132.

43. Colm Luibheid, *Pseudo-Dionysius: The Areopagite* (New York: Paulist, 1985), 141.

In the end Meninger adopted a simple method culled from *The Cloud of Unknowing*, advising the practioner to "sit relaxed and quiet" and to select a simple prayer word. "Contemplatives rarely pray in words but . . . a word of one syllable is more suited to the spiritual nature of this work than longer ones." Introducing the word into the mind, you are reminded, "Do not to use clever logic to examine or explain this word [or] to ponder its ramifications." Avoiding reflection and "analytical thought," you enter the "Cloud of Unknowing," the apophatic, contemplative dimension beyond words, thoughts, and emotions. When distractions do occur, the formula is to "reject the thought and experience of all created things but especially . . . yourself." In this way you "will find a naked knowing and feeling of your own being still remains between you and your God." The method is gentle: "be careful never to strain your body or spirit." In fact, a concentrative approach to the apophatic is unlikely to work because "anyone who presumes to approach this lofty mountain of contemplative prayer through sheer brute force will be driven off with stones."[44]

Years later, Keating would distill the elements of this prayer, with other influences, into guidelines for Centering Prayer:

1. Choose a sacred word as the symbol of your intention to consent to God's presence and action within.
2. Sitting comfortably and with eyes closed, settle briefly and silently introduce the sacred word as the symbol of your consent to God's presence and action within.
3. When you become aware of thoughts, return ever-so-gently to the sacred word.
4. At the end of the prayer period, remain in silence with eyes closed for a couple of minutes.[45]

---

44. William Johnston, ed., *The Cloud of Unknowing and the Book of Privy Counseling* (Garden City, N.Y.: Image Books, 1973), 55–56, 94–95, 102–3, 107.

45. Keating, *Intimacy with God*, 64.

Meninger called his distillation "The Prayer of the Cloud" and taught it in the monastery guest house. In 1976 Pennington, invited to conduct retreats for Roman Catholic religious superiors, refined Meninger's method further and retreatants named it Centering Prayer, perhaps inspired by Thomas Merton's use of the term. Keating began teaching this method after his 1981 retirement as abbot. Since that time Keating has continued to teach and refine his approach to Centering Prayer. While Centering Prayer is not *lectio divina*, it facilitates the transition from discursive and affective prayer into contemplation. It "relates to Lectio Divina as a discipline designed to correct what hinders or prevents us from moving from simplified affective prayer into contemplation."[46]

In those early days the monks of Spencer Abbey realized that this simple method allowed an experience of the contemplative dimension immediately, without years of monastic practice of *lectio divina*. Two tenets of conventional wisdom about contemplative prayer were challenged: first, that it requires a monastic milieu for its practice; second, that one must move from discursive meditation to affective prayer and to contemplation only when called by God. The monks realized that God has something else in mind after all: people in active life were as likely to thrive in this prayer as monastics or priests. Clearly, contemplative prayer was not solely the fruit of many years of disciplined mental prayer. It could be experienced in the beginning of a prayer life and provide reinforcement of the spiritual purification process:

> Why is it so hard to imagine a person, even an "inexperienced" Christian, being moved by the contemplative gifts of wisdom, understanding, and knowledge while praying? It is not that hard for God.[47]

Union through Purification: The Three-Fold Way and Divine Therapy

KEATING IS FOND of describing what happens as a result of a commitment to a regular practice of Centering Prayer: *Ad lumen per*

46. Ibid., 122.
47. Ibid., 123.

crucem ("to illumination through the cross"). Indeed, the crucifixion of the false self is an ongoing process of purification facilitated and accelerated by Centering Prayer.

When the Fathers described this process, they depicted it in terms of demons assaulting the soul in spiritual warfare. There could be no more striking example than Anthony of the Desert locked in an Egyptian tomb physically battling the spirits of Fornication and Anger. Pseudo-Dionysius saw it as an internal process, a movement from cataphatic to apophatic prayer: from purification (*katharsis*), to contemplation (*theoria*), and then to union (*henosis*). As the monastic experience grew, writers sought to place the purification process in a "safer" environment than Anthony's demon-infested tomb. They argued that it should take place within scriptural prayer—in the presence of God in the Word. In the thirteenth century Bonaventure articulated purification as a threefold way:

> A threefold spiritual interpretation, that is, moral, allegorical, and mystical. Now, this threefold interpretation corresponds to a threefold hierarchical action: PURGATION, ILLUMINATION, and PERFECT UNION. Purgation leads to peace, illumination to truth, and perfective union to love . . . for upon the proper understanding of these three states are founded both the understanding of all Scriptures and the right to eternal life.
>
> Know also that there are three approaches to this triple way: reading with meditation; prayer; contemplation."[48]

Keating sees the process of purification beginning in the allegorical sense of Scripture when we see that Scripture is not just story and moral subtext but realize that it is actually about ourselves. This personal identification with the texts of the scripture triggers catharsis. For example, seeing ourselves as Israel, captive not of Egypt but of sin, following Moses into the desert to confront the consequence of sin, to find a promised land, the freedom from sin—this can stimulate a self-disclosure that allows us to confront the darker side of our personality in God's presence.

---

48. José de Vinck, trans., *The Works of Bonaventure: Cardinal, Seraphic Doctor, and Saint* (Paterson, N.J.: St. Anthony Guild Press, 1960), 63.

The allegorical level of Scripture involves emptying the unconscious of junk—that is, the emotional damage that has been done to us since early childhood. It has to be emptied out before the experience of divine union can be fully achieved, before the true self can begin to motivate us rather than the false self.[49]

Centering Prayer clearly emerged directly from *lectio divina* and two millenia of contemplative prayer, but what should one expect from a prayer method that is nonconceptual and nondiscursive by nature? After years of teaching Centering Prayer and praying with practitioners, Keating began to notice a pattern of purification and healing; he eventually termed it "divine therapy." Articulating this process based on a paradigm of contemporary psychology is one of Keating's unique and most important contributions to today's renewal of contemplative prayer.

Keating sees divine therapy as having four distinct "moments." First, sitting in Centering Prayer, one consents to the presence and action of God within by practicing the simple method, which gently establishes "an attitude of waiting upon the Lord with loving attentiveness." This results in a second moment of rest, comfort, and peace characterized by spiritual attentiveness with physiological conditions that indicate a state of rest deeper than sleep.[50] The purgative action of the third moment begins in this deep spiritual rest:

> The hardpan of defense mechanisms around the emotional weeds of a lifetime begins to soften, the body's extraordinary capacity for health revives, and the psyche begins to release its waste materials. Our awareness during prayer becomes a channel of evacuation similar to the evacuation channels of the physical body. The psyche then starts to disgorge the undigested emotional material of a lifetime in what might be called an attack of "psychic nausea."[51]

---

49. Keating, *Intimacy with God*, 50.

50. Herbert Benson, *Beyond the Relaxation Response: How to Harness the Healing Power of Your Personal Beliefs* (New York: Times Books, 1984), 5–131.

51. Keating, *Intimacy with God*, 78.

In this third moment, which Keating terms "the unloading of the unconscious," one experiences a bombardment of thoughts and feelings that surge into our consciousness without any relationship to the present or past. As these raw, unconscious energies pass through our awareness, they are removed in a fourth moment:

> Having carried this emotional pain for twenty or thirty years (or longer), the evacuation process may be extremely painful, but if it is prepared for by the discipline of a practice like Centering Prayer on a daily basis, then the trust in the Divine Therapist is there to enable us to handle it.[52]

Trust in the Holy Spirit is essential as the decision of what is healed first is not a conscious undertaking. The process is left for the Holy Spirit, the "Divine Therapist," to function as diagnostician, apothecarian, and therapist. There is no effort to rationally examine the quality or source of the releasing emotions as in psychotherapy. There is no attempt to dwell emotionally on the release as in Eugene Gendlin's focusing methodology.[53] There is only the simple instruction to return ever-so-gently to the sacred word and initiate the cycle again. Evagrius describes how the purification is directed not by a conscious decision but by an internal process:

> Just as the soul perceives its sick members as it operates by means of the body, so also the spirit recognizes its own powers as it puts its own faculties into operation and it is able to discover the healing commandment through experiencing the impediments to its free movement.[54]

The long-term implication of committing to the practice of Centering Prayer is spiritual freedom. Patterns of conditioned emotional responses, repressions and "emotional programs for happiness" are diminished and eventually extinguished. The deeper the "divine archeologist" (as Keating calls God in this

52. Ibid., 79.
53. Eugene T. Gendlin, *Focusing* (New York: Everest House, 1978).
54. Evagrius, *Praktikos,* 36–37.

matter) digs into our false self, the more raw and primitive the release might become. The evacuation leaves space for a greater degree of spiritual freedom and attentiveness. This is the freedom from the consequences of original and personal sin. When the illusion and weakness of will are banished. what remains for Keating is a state of divine union.

Transforming Union to Divine Union: From Apatheia to Agape

THE DESERT FATHERS named this state of spiritual perfection *apatheia*, which is sometimes misunderstood as indifference or detachment. In fact, it is a state of spiritual freedom where life is unburdened by the emotional obsessions characteristic of the false self:

> The experience of the transforming union is a way of being in the world that enables us to live daily life with the invincible conviction of continuous union with God. It is a new way of being in the world, a way of transcending everything in the world without leaving it.[55]

After the fruits of contemplative prayer are fully integrated, the soul remains in the presence of God, whether we are awake or asleep. One has moved from consent to the presence and action of God within to surrender and union with God's presence. This transformation involves the entire person, restructuring spiritual and psychological faculties:

> The proof of *apatheia* is had when the spirit begins to see its own light, when it remains in a state of tranquillity in the presence of the images it has during sleep and when it maintains its calm as it beholds the affairs of life. . . . The soul which has *apatheia* is not simply the one which is not disturbed by changing events but the one which remains unmoved at the memory of them as well.[56]

---

55. Thomas Keating, *Invitation to Lose: The Way of Christian Contemplation* (Rockport Mass.: Element Books, 1992), 101.

56. Evagrius, *Praktikos*, 33–34.

Out of the experience of union of the soul with God's presence grows an even greater intimacy, a unity where "God and our true self are not separate. Though we are not God, God and our true self are the same thing."[57] This state of unity with God is a marriage of love. "*Agape* is the progeny of *apatheia*. *Apatheia* is the very flower of *ascesis*."[58]

Such descriptions in their psychological precision sound more like a state of consciousness than Christian love. Indeed, they can erroneously set up an expectation of spiritual perfection that is distinctly non-Christian:

> The fallacy I detect here is the tendency to identify particular experiences with certain stages of growth, and in particular to identify a certain kind of prayer, a contemplative type of prayer such as Centering Prayer, with a certain advanced stage of progress, and to make a project of its attainment.[59]

The Christian experience of unity with God is not a state of consciousness or awareness but a state of love where the soul participates in the true nature of the Trinity and infinite love. As William of St. Thierry stated:

> The stages of love are not like rungs of a ladder. The Soul does not leave the lesser love behind it as moves onward to the more perfect. All the degrees of love work together as one.[60]

Living in *agape,* Keating asserts, we begin to express the Beatitudes, to fully commit ourselves to the needs and rights of the entire human family. Indeed, he sees this as the first moment where we can fully express the love of Christ:

> We are free to devote ourselves to the needs of others. We are present to people at the deepest level and perceive the presence of Christ suffering in them. We long to share with them something of the inner freedom we have been given, but without anxiety and without trying to change them or obtain anything from them.[61]

---

57. Keating, *Open Mind, Open Heart,* 127.

58. Evagrius, *Praktikos*. 36.

59. Pennington, *Centering Prayer*, 112.

60. William of St. Thierry, *On Contemplating God: Prayer, Meditations*, Sister Penelope, trans. (Spencer, Mass.: Cistercian Publications, 1971).

61. Keating, *Invitation to Love*, 102.

Put simply, contemplative prayer evokes service and commitment, not withdrawal and privatization.

Centering Prayer is neither new nor an invention. It arises from the ladder of prayer—from discursive to contemplative prayer—known and experienced by all with a life of prayer. It is drawn from the Christian contemplative tradition and has roots in the Hebrew Bible. As such, the work of Thomas Keating, Basil Pennington, and William Meninger stands solidly in the mainstream; they also comprise the vanguard of renewal and restoration of the contemplative dimension of the gospel, offering perhaps one contemporary answer to Jesus's plaint, "If salt has lost its taste, how can its saltiness be restored" (Matt. 5:13b).

Although there has been a significant reception for Centering Prayer among laity, it is only now finding general acceptance among clergy and theologians. Wise counsel is found in Diogenes Allen's advice on renewal:

> For all the inadequacies of the church, it continues to be blessed with divine grace, a constructive vision, and a genuine strength. We as its representatives have a great calling: to be alert to every spiritual awakening in the church, to see such awakenings as not merely human phenomena, and to nurture them with all the wisdom we can muster.[62]

Ecclesiastical, academic, and lay acceptance of the Christian contemplative tradition, no matter how affirmative, will not alone restore the apophatic dimension of prayer to the church. It is a matter of praxis. As Keating says continually, "Just pray."

---

62. Allen, *Spiritual Awakenings*, 5.

4

An Episcopalian Perspective on Centering Prayer

THOMAS R. WARD, JR.

> The Spirit helps us in our weakness; for we do not know how to pray as we ought, but that very Spirit intercedes (for us) with sighs too deep for words. (Rom. 8:26)

Very few of us feel that we know how to pray as we ought. But we do know what it is to sigh, to yearn for a deeper and more intimate relation with the One whom Jesus taught us to call *Abba,* Father. And it is good to hear that our own sighs may be our participation in the sighing of the Spirit, helping us in our weakness, as we seek to claim our identity as daughters and sons of God.

In our day many are bringing their sighing hearts before God in Centering Prayer. But what is Centering Prayer? Where does it come from? How does one practice this discipline? And how does one find support when keeping this discipline becomes difficult? I hope to answer these questions, among others, in this article by relating something of my own pilgrimage.

I.

AS A BORN and reared Episcopalian, I heard the language of *The Book of Common Prayer* from my earliest days: the music of its set prayers enchanted my soul. While I still have many of the prayers of *The Book of Common Prayer 1928* by heart, one prayer in particular has stayed with me in a sustaining way over the years:

> O God of peace, who hast taught us that in returning and rest we shall be saved, in quietness and in confidence shall be our strength: By the might of thy Spirit lift us, we pray thee, to thy presence, where we may be still and know that thou art God; through Jesus Christ our Lord. *Amen.*[1]

Peace, rest, quietness, confidence, strength, presence, stillness, knowledge—these words, even out of context, have a tranquil solidity of their own. In this prayer they call the pray-er to the still point in his turning world. Over the years and through the education I was privileged to receive, I learned that these words have deep scriptural roots, primarily in the Hebrew Scriptures: in the prophets (Isa. 30:15, for instance) and in the psalms (Ps. 46:11), among others.

The word *knowledge* in particular has powerful connotations. To know and be known in the biblical sense is to be in a relationship that involves the whole person: body, mind, and spirit. The same Hebrew verb that describes intimacy with Yahweh also describes sexual intercourse between a man and a woman.

Psalm 139 still speaks to me as it spoke to me in the early days of my formation:

> Lord, you have searched me out and know me; *
> you know my sitting down and my rising up;
> you discern my thoughts from afar . . .
>
> You press upon me behind and before*
> and lay your hand upon me.
>
> Such knowledge is too wonderful and excellent for me*
> it is so high that I cannot attain to it.

---

1. This prayer continues to appear in *The Book of Common Prayer* (New York: Church Hymnal Corporation, 1979), 832. (Hereafter, *BCP*.)

> Where can I go then from your Spirit?*
> where can I flee from your presence? . . .
>
> If I say, "Surely the darkness will cover me,*
> and the light around me turn to night,"
>
> Darkness is not dark to you;
> the night is as bright as the day;*
> darkness and light to you are both alike.[2]

I was both attracted to and frightened of knowing and being known by the God who has searched me out and known me, and I still am.

Later, while I continued my studies, I learned that the New Testament describes Jesus' relation to God in equally intimate terms. In the Gospel of John the author portrays the relation between God and Jesus in the language of knowing and being known (10:15). He has Jesus say that the one who knows him will know the One whom he calls "Father" (14:7). This author uses the language of "abiding" (15:5) and mutual indwelling (17:21, 23) to describe the relationship between the "Father," the "Son," and the believer.[3]

What struck me as I delved more deeply into the gospel tradition of Jesus and his prayer was the consistency with which he prayed to the God of Israel as his Father. In Mark we are told that Jesus used the word *Abba* in his prayer (14:36). This is the Aramaic word for an intimate father–son relationship. It lies behind the ordinary Greek term *pater,* which is the word that Gospel writers most often use in having Jesus refer to his "Father."[4] When the disciples asked Jesus to teach them to pray, he begins with this intimate word (Luke 11:2). Jesus brings them into the relation that he experienced intensely at his baptism (e.g., Mark 1:9–11).[5] In this passage Mark tells us that Jesus "saw the heavens torn apart and the Spirit" descending upon him.

---

2. *BCP,* 794.

3. Raymond E. Brown, trans./ed., *The Gospel According to John I–XII* 2d ed. (Garden City, N.Y.: Doubleday, 1985–86), 510.

4. John Koenig, *Rediscovering New Testament Prayer: Boldness and Blessing in the Name of Jesus* (New York: Harper, 1992), 18.

5. Bernard J. Cooke, *God's Beloved: Jesus' Experience of the Transcendent* (Philadelphia: Trinity Press International, 1992), 12.

As I entered parish ministry, I noticed the Trinitarian character of liturgical language.[6] This drove me back to my study to discern the relation between Jesus' prayer to his *Abba* as recorded in the Gospel tradition and the church's experience of prayer. What I saw was that earlier strands of the New Testament used Trinitarian language (2 Cor. 13:14). In fact, more than once Paul used Aramaic and Greek words together for Father, words that Mark shows Jesus using, and he links their use to the Spirit at work in the believer: "When we cry 'Abba! Father!' it is that very Spirit bearing witness with our spirit that we are children of God, and if children, then heirs, heirs of God and joint heirs with Christ" (Rom. 8:15b–17; cf. Gal. 4:6).

John Koenig comments on these passages in the following way:

> These passages show us the very wellspring of New Testament spirituality. We may, indeed the Spirit impels us, to pray with the same love word that Jesus used. And we are led to address Jesus as the true ruler of our world. Because Jesus' life before God in his ministry is vindicated by the resurrection, and because the God who raised Jesus graciously unites us with him through the Holy Spirit, we are caught up in nothing less than the dynamism of the Trinity itself. [7]

I began to see what *The Book of Common Prayer* means when it describes Christian prayer as "response to God the Father, through Jesus Christ, in the power of the Holy Spirit."[8] And so I saw that the intimate knowledge of God that I had first glimpsed in that prayer "For Quiet Confidence" in *The Book of Common Prayer* was the birthright of all Christians and that it was at the heart of our tradition. Then I wondered why I had heard and read so little about this gift and why what I had read made it seem so unusual and esoteric.

The writings of Thomas Merton[9] helped me understand something of the history of contemplative prayer in our tradition,

---

6. For example, see *BCP,* 362–63.

7. Koenig, *Rediscovering New Testament Prayer,* 27.

8. *BCP,* 856.

9. Thomas Merton, *Contemplative Prayer* (Garden City, N.Y.: Image Books, 1971).

as did the work of Louis Bouyer.[10] But it was Thomas Keating who traced the ebb and flow of contemplative prayer in Christianity in a way that helped me understand that my confusion was not idiosyncratic but communal: the Church as a whole had lost one of the great gifts from its Lord and was in the process of reclaiming it. This is not the place to make that case in detail. But a few sentences from Keating make the essential point:

> A positive attitude toward contemplation characterized the first fifteen centuries of the Christian era. Unfortunately, a negative attitude has prevailed from the sixteenth century onward. . . . The post-Reformation teaching opposed to contemplation was the direct opposite of the earlier tradition. That tradition, taught uninterruptedly or the first fifteen centuries, held that contemplation is the normal evolution of a genuine spiritual life and is open to all Christians.[11]

Finally, I had a name for what I had experienced through that prayer "For Quiet Confidence": contemplation.

II.

FOR MOST OF my life I associated "contemplation" with monks, nuns, and monasteries—with good reason. For me it was a word that referred to the cloistered discipline of super-Christians. I did not see any connection between my own attraction to the prayer "For Quiet Confidence" and my hunger to know God as I was already known, on the one hand, and "contemplation," on the other. But gradually that changed. The more I read Merton, Keating, and Basil Pennington[12] and kept the discipline of Centering Prayer twenty minutes twice a day, the more I sensed that the silence before God I felt drawn to might be given the

---

10. Louis Bouyer, *A History of Christian Spirituality,* vol.1: *The Spirituality of the New Testament and the Fathers* (New York: The Seabury Press, 1982).

11. Thomas Keating, *Open Mind, Open Heart: The Contemplative Dimension of the Gospel* (New York: Amity House, 1986), 26.

12. M. Basil Pennington, *Centering Prayer: Renewing an Ancient Christian Prayer Form* (Garden City, N.Y.: Image Books, 1982).

name "contemplation." Of particular help in this regard was the affirmation by these writers, among others, that contemplation was not just for monks and nuns but "is the normal evolution of a genuine spiritual life . . . open to all Christians."[13]

Moreover, I began to see further traces of contemplation in my own Episcopal heritage. For instance, the section on "Prayer and Worship" in the Catechism of *The Book of Common Prayer 1979* clearly acknowledges this strand of the tradition:

> Q. What is prayer?
> A. Prayer is responding to God, by thought and by deeds, with or without words.
>
> Q. What is Christian prayer?
> A. Christian prayer is response to God the Father, through Jesus Christ, in the power of the Holy Spirit.
>
> Q. What are the principal kinds of prayer?
> A. The principal kinds of prayer are adoration, praise, thanksgiving, penitence, oblation, intercession, and petition.
>
> Q. What is adoration?
> A. Adoration is the lifting up of the heart and mind to God, asking nothing but to enjoy God's presence.
>
> Q. Why do we praise God?
> A. We praise God, not to obtain anything, but because God's being draws praise from us.[14]

"Prayer . . . without words": that is contemplation. "Lifting up of the heart and mind to God, asking for nothing but to enjoy God's presence"—that too is contemplation. "God's being draws praise from us." That is what I was experiencing. Contemplation is more than these traces, but it includes them. My worlds were beginning to come together.

What drew them together was the practice of Centering Prayer.

III.

WHAT, THEN, IS Centering Prayer? What is contemplative prayer?

---

13. Keating, *Open Mind, Open Heart,* 26.
14. *BCP,* 856–57.

And what is the relation between them? Thomas Keating answers these questions in detail.

Contemplative prayer first:

> Contemplative prayer is a process of interior transformation, a conversation initiated by God and leading, if we consent, to divine union.[15]

Then Centering Prayer and the relation between these two:

> Centering Prayer is an effort to renew the teaching the Christian tradition on contemplative prayer. It is an attempt to present that tradition in an up-to-date form and to put a certain order and method into it. Like the word *contemplation,* the term *Centering Prayer* has come to have a variety of meanings. For the sake of clarity it seems best to reserve the term *Centering Prayer* for the specific method of preparing for the gift of contemplation . . . and to return to the traditional term *contemplative prayer* when describing its development under the more direct inspiration of the Spirit.[16]

This distinction is subtle and may appear meaningless to those readers new to this conversation. In another place Keating describes Centering Prayer "as the first rung on the ladder of contemplative prayer, which rises step by step to union with God."[17] So Centering Prayer gives us a way to begin to respond to God's initiative. It puts us on the ladder. It gives us a method of being present to God in spite of the many obstacles within us that block our effort to be responsively present. Centering Prayer offers us the hope of interior transformation leading to the divine union which is ours through baptism.

Following Hosea, Teresa of Ávila, Thomas à Kempis, and others, Keating compares our relationship to God to a loving relationship with another human being. In particular, he sees our relationship to Christ going through four stages of increasing intimacy: from acquaintanceship, to friendliness, to friendship, to union. We begin by meeting another (acquaintanceship). If we sense an attraction and commonalty, we might spend more time together (friendliness). Should we find an even deeper pull, we

15. *Keating, Open Mind, Open Heart,* 4.
16. Ibid., 3–4.
17. Ibid.

might commit ourselves to a relationship of fidelity over time (friendship). Then, if this commitment deepens, we might find this commitment to be the center of our world, so much so that we find ourselves at one with the other (union). Courtship leading to marriage is the most common human analogy.

In terms of the Catechism in *The Book of Common Prayer,* Centering Prayer gives us a wordless way[18] to respond to God's invitation to a covenantal relationship. It is a means of consenting to God's being—which draws praise from us—a way of allowing the Spirit to lift our hearts and minds to God, asking nothing but to enjoy God's presence (adoration).

IV.

PRAY. PRAY. PRAY. It is one thing to read an article such as this about Centering Prayer. It is quite another to practice this discipline. And it is the practice that gives meaning to these words.

Keating recommends keeping this discipline twenty minutes twice a day.[19] It takes most of us at least twenty minutes to establish the necessary level of interior silence and to get beyond our superficial thoughts. If we keep this discipline first early in the morning, we will need a second time of silence in God by the late afternoon. Keating compares this need to keeping a certain level of antibiotic in our bloodstream to counter an infection. In this analogy it is our thoughts that are the infection; our attachment to them draws us from the presence of God as we go about our lives in the world.

And it is in our active lives that we should look for the fruits of our praying, not in the time of prayer. During the prayer as we notice thoughts entering our consciousness and then return to the sacred word, we establish a rhythm of consent to God's presence and action within us that continues as we move into our daily lives. We find that we are more appropriately detached from

---

18. Centering Prayer is not altogether "wordless." It makes use of a "sacred word" as a means of returning to God's presence and action within. But this is the only use of words in the practice of Centering Prayer.

19. See the appendix, "The Method of Centering Prayer," of this volume for specific details on this process.

persons and issues to which we were formerly attached and that we are enabled to let go of disquieting distractions. As a consequence we are more present to what we are given to do.

Over time we notice in ourselves an increase in the fruits of the Spirit that are listed in Galatians: "love, joy, peace, patience, kindness, generosity, faithfulness, gentleness, and self-control" (Gal. 5:22). More than likely, others will comment on these traits before we notice them in ourselves. Most of us notice an increasing attraction to silence, solitude, and simplicity of life. Some persons report an increased capacity to listen to other people, a less judgmental attitude, and an increasing acceptance of others. In the last parish I served I noticed that those who practiced Centering Prayer became more intentional in lay pastoral care and in ministry to God's poor through the parish.

This emphasis on the fruits of the Spirit runs the risk of presenting the Spirit as if She works mechanically through the prayer, as if there is some one-to-one correspondence between practicing this discipline and doing God's work in the world. Far from it, as with all true prayer, Centering Prayer is personal. It is our response to the One who initiates a relationship with each of us. What happens to us and in us through this way of praying is as unique as each of us is. The God and Father of our Lord Jesus Christ takes each of us as we are, where we are, and calls us into a deeper relation with him and with others through him. That is and will always remain mysteriously personal.

An example: A clergy colleague of mine began practicing Centering Prayer after years of struggling with a propensity to overfunction at work. He described himself as "a recovering workaholic." As a child he thought he was being judged in terms of external achievements in the world: grades at school, accomplishments in sports, and work productivity outside the classroom. Internalizing these expectations, he judged himself against an ever-escalating standard of achievement. He came to realize that he saw God as a judge who expected high achievement and held him accountable even to his own unrealistic standards.

Years of psychotherapy helped him understand his condition, but he found he could change very little about his behavior.

To himself he would recite, "I do not do what I want, but I do the very thing I hate. . . . I can will what is right, but I cannot do it" (Rom. 7:15, 18). Even though he prayed about his condition without ceasing, he found that his dilemma only deepened. Prayer became another task on his "to do" list, another source of guilt. He discovered Centering Prayer, he said, "when I was near burning out."

In describing his experience of Centering Prayer, he said it was as if he had found a place to rest in the silence before God. The voice that told him that he ought to be busy and active doing one thing or another would emerge. He would notice it, and as soon as he noticed it, he would return to the sacred word. He said that he would have a sense of peace when he ended the prayer period. Even more important to him, however, was his attitude at work; he was able to distinguish the *more* important from the *less* important, to discern what was a real act of service from a compulsive need to be needed, or from a fear of failure if he did not respond to every impulse. He said that he did not feel perpetually guilty as he had before and that he had a sense that he was doing what God wanted him to do.

This report has the ring of authenticity. And it is not unlike many other stories I have heard from those who practice Centering Prayer and much like my own experience as well. There is something about practicing this discipline that breathes life into the words of the Scriptures and the tradition: ". . . it is no longer I who live but it is Christ who lives in me. And the life I now live in the flesh I live by faith in the Son of God, who loved me and gave himself for me" (Gal. 2:20).

V.

"TWENTY MINUTES, TWICE a day. That's not much time. Keeping this discipline ought to be easy for those who say they love God and want to grow in knowledge and love of God." So we say. So I have said. But even if we begin with good intentions and much enthusiasm, we may find all kinds of reasons not to follow through. Old habits are deeply engrained; introducing a new pattern can constellate powerful resistances. Some of us discover that we do not, in fact, want to pray as much as we thought we did.

Thomas Keating recommends a weekly support group for those attempting to keep this discipline. Such a group reinforces our original intention and encourages our fidelity through the rough times, which aresure to come. It provides accountability and an opportunity for continuing education. *Open Mind, Open Heart* offers suggestions in structuring such a group.[20]

The last parish I served provided such a support group for over six years. It continues to this day. We found that many persons both in and outside the parish were interested in learning about Centering Prayer. While a few of those who learned the guidelines did not continue with the prayer or the group, most did. And many of these found the prayer central to their ministry in the world. One woman called it "a preparation for and an extension of the Eucharist." As the rector of that parish, I drew deep strength from praying with other members of the parish in the silence.

VI.

WHILE FEW IF any of us feel we know how to pray as we ought, most of us yearn for a deeper relation with God. Centering Prayer is one way to pray. It is grounded in Scripture and has a rich history in the Christian tradition. Moreover, many persons in our day are finding this discipline a way to respond to God that is in keeping with their lives in the local parish church and their service in the world. It is the Spirit praying in us with sighs too deep for words.

---

20. Thomas Keating, *Open Mind, Open Heart,* 135–36.

5 ❖

Taizé and Centering Prayer: An Innovative Collaboration

THOMAS NEENAN, DAVID WALTON MILLER, AND GUSTAVE REININGER

Many who practice Centering Prayer have expressed a need to liturgically celebrate the contemplative dimension of the gospel that they experience through contemplative prayer. Often a contemplative Eucharist, a quiet intimate service that includes a period of Centering Prayer, addresses this yearning. As Contemplative Outreach grows in ecumenical and international dimensions, multidenominational sharing of Eucharist more and more becomes an issue of great sensitivity and respect for the different theological traditions within Christianity. The historical conflicts surrounding sharing communion become a serious consideration as an ecumenical balance is sought. Which liturgy from which Christian theological tradition is always a principle question.

Many have heard of Taizé and the style of service attributed to this ecumenical monastic community in the small Burgundian village of Taizé, France. Popes, Orthodox Metropolitans, and archbishops of Canterbury have made pilgrimages. A visit to Taizé is almost a rite of passage for European Christian youth. And now more and more American youth church groups make the journey to this sacred place—a testament to prayer as the common ground of Christian unity. As interest in Taizé spread here in America (primarily on the fringes of Roman Catholic and Episcopal parishes), many music directors in mainstream parishes wondered if there wasn't something useful in the music for their customary liturgies.

At the Parish of St. Matthew (Episcopal) in Pacific Palisades, California, the Centering Prayer program and the music program conspired to radically adapt the conventional Taizé service to provide an introduction and celebration of the contemplative dimension of prayer. Those who already practice Centering Prayer and those who wish to learn more about this approach to Christian contemplative prayer and the heritage from which it is drawn seem to agree that this service is one of the most profound participatory liturgies they have ever experienced. Indeed, this contemplative adaptation of the Taizé service appears to work well in situations where there are concerns about shared communion.

Tom Neenan, St. Matthew's music director, attracted to the simplicity and the participatory nature of the Taizé chants, had begun using them in the Sunday morning Eucharist at St. Matthew's but with only limited success. The unfamiliarity of the Taizé chant left most of the congregation in the listening posture, not participating. It also seemed the busyness of Sunday morning worship is, at least at churches like St. Matthew's, antithetical to the contemplative and somewhat open-ended nature of a Taizé service.

By 1995, the growth in the Centering Prayer program at St. Matthew's was remarkable as over a thousand participants per annum came to the parish's Centering Prayer offerings. Trinity Grants Program of Trinity Episcopal Church of New York recognized the spiritual value of Centering Prayer to the entire Episcopal church and offered a substantial grant to St. Matthew's to help make Centering Prayer more available in the Anglican communion in America and beyond. With this support the program entered a new phase of growth and began attracting Christians of many denominations and attitudes—from ardent evangelicals to mainline churchgoers to those who had sought enlightenment in Eastern prayer methods and wanted to negotiate a repatriation to Christianity. This diversity, and the emerging liturgical needs it occasioned, spurred ongoing discussion on how to introduce the Taizé chants into Centering Prayer retreat days. The easiest solution was to merely insert a period of Centering Prayer in the middle of a shortened Taizé service. However, Centering Prayer is silent and not a prayer of singing and liturgical ritual. Many persons who share Centering Prayer know the deep spiritual bonding of this prayer of silence, but have never experienced the special bonding—indeed the expression of Centering Prayer's ecclesial fruits—which liturgical worship can effect. To experience Centering Prayer in a continuum with other forms of prayer, with chanting and vocal prayer, opened everyone involved to a profound spiritual integration.

The following summer, Tom went on sabbatical to France and had a life-changing experience taking an intensive course in Gregorian semiology at St. Pierre's Abbey, in Solesmes. He tacked on a visit to Taizé but was not prepared for what he encountered.

As he drove up the hill to Taizé on a July evening the first thing that struck him was the enormous crowd. He wondered if he was indeed at a monastery or had happened on a French Woodstock. Sixteen- to twenty-year-olds were wandering around hand in hand, drinking soda, and being rowdy. But when the bell for evening service rang, there was a near stampede to the large "church"—a barnlike structure which obviously had been added on to many times and which featured, among other things, bad acoustics, uncomfortable and inadequate seating, faulty ventilation, and intermittent amplification for the "song leaders." This was Taizé?

In spite of the musical leadership served up by Brother Organist, Brother Guitarist, assembled volunteer (teen) vocalists, and what appeared to be a Romanian pilgrim who had packed an oboe at the last minute, the assembled masses—hot and sweaty from the 90-plus degree heat of the day—began to chant. By the third or fourth repetition nearly all of the 6,000 persons assembled were participating. The music had a beat; there was enough accompaniment to keep everyone on pitch and moving; people were improvising, harmonizing, descanting, and singing in ten different languages! It was a Christian Dionysian God-fest—a primal worship experience, not frequently encountered in Christian contexts.

As a musician Tom learned several important lessons that night: (1) strong, assertive musical leadership is critical (at Taizé, the musical leadership is not always of a stellar quality but it is, for the most part, assertive and well amplified); (2) the music of Taizé is not always quiet and reflective but often jubilant and rambunctious; and (3) the music is an adjunct (a kind of vestibule) to a movement of spirit within: a contemplative dimension that then turns outward, into exuberant praise and adoration. But how to translate the qualities of this experience with 6,000 pilgrims to a well-to-do parish in a Los Angeles suburb?

Upon returning Tom met with St. Matthew's rector, David Walton Miller, and Gus Reininger to design what they hoped would be a new and meaningful service. Each had his own wish list.

Tom wanted good, strong musical leadership and a more diverse palette of sounds. This meant training a choir in the chants and working out instrumental orchestrations. He also wanted the distribution of tapers to the congregation, which at Taizé seemed like a Milky Way of nighttime candlelight.

David Miller, remembering services at Mercy Center in Burlingame, California, wanted an icon or some tangible visual focus for the congregation. He suggested an "adoration of the cross," where participants would voluntarily leave their seats and walk into the chancel to sit at the foot of the cross, to touch it, kneel or stand, near the symbol of the paschal mystery. He insisted on not having a sermon or any other distractions, particularly anyone calling a play-by-play of the service. He encouraged well-directed liturgical movements that a congregation could follow without verbal prompts, so that the silent "container" of the service would be maintained.

Gus wanted Centering Prayer at the heart of the service. But there were several problems: First, of those who might attend, many might not yet know the practice of Centering Prayer, which takes six to twelve weeks to learn. Moreover, only twelve minutes were available within the service. So Gus suggested silent prayer with Scripture instead: *lectio divina,* historically a private prayer practice from the monastic milieu, but which now comes in many varieties. More often it is composed of reflective or discursive prayer, complemented by "talking and sharing," which keeps the prayer on a conceptual or affective level. This certainly keeps the prayer active and not receptive, which is the essential nature of Contemplative Prayer. To offer a taste of silence would require a "dynamic" which would facilitate a movement into contemplative prayer. Those with an established practice of Centering Prayer know its effectiveness in the transition from active forms of prayer to receptive prayer, moving into Contemplation. For others, this first experience of silent prayer might be an enticement to learn Centering Prayer or to respect it as part of an integrated continuum of prayer.

The following are the basic outlines of the service that was developed and shared with numerous parishes around the country.

Musical Considerations

IN ADDITION TO the normal Taizé chants, we use some of Bill Robert's fine "Taizéttes" (as he calls them), Gregorian chants, and some of Tom Neenan's original settings. Great care was taken to select chants which support the different dynamics of the service—movements from active to receptive forms of prayer.

At St. Matthew's a goodly number of the thirty-voice choir usually attend the service. Singers and instrumentalists from other parishes frequently join the choir and "band." It took us several rehearsals and two services before the well-disciplined choir was able to let go and experience the spontaneous, improvisational quality of the Taizé chant arrangements.

Instrumentally, the guideline is to keep things simple but to encourage whatever works to deepen the contemplative dimension. Our "band" usually consists of two synthesizers, a twelve-string guitar, multiple reed instruments (played by one person), a cello, Tibetan gong, handbells, piano, or organ.

Liturgical Preparations

PEOPLE ENTER AND are given a printed program with an order of service and a taper. The lights are low enough to suggest a contemplative atmosphere, but not too low to render the program unreadable.

We start in a semidark church with Centering Prayer for thirty minutes prior to the service so that people arrive in an environment of silent prayer. There is no socializing, just a plunging into an atmosphere of profound quiet and peace, which seems especially noticeable to those who are new to a prayer of silence. Sometimes the initial uneasiness with no talking expresses itself in squirming and whispering but eventual the silence wins out, and usually ushers in a new experience of God's silent presence. Then from this well of silence the service emerges. There is no formal process or "start," just very quite tones arising from the silence.

For a focal point we use a simple cross[1] (without corpus), sitting in a floor mount in the center of the chancel, which is cleared of all other accoutrements—altar, chairs, table, and ambo. Before the cross is a box of sand in which is placed four or five lighted tapers; but ample enough for a couple of hundred tapers.

Half the choir (in street clothes) is gathered with the instrumentalists with the other half sitting in the congregation as "ringers" to encourage participatory singing.

Ideally, this is a presiderless service with the visual focus on the cross as an active symbol of the internal experience. However, congregations seem to need to have someone who appears to be facilitating the service, if only to relieve them of the burden of wondering what is coming next. The rubrics are designed to be followed without verbal instructions. Each chant is usually singable without music or lyrics after the third repetition. We achieve this

---

1. The particular cross at St. Matthew's is one of the few charred remnants of a fire that leveled the original church. In itself it is a powerful paschal symbol. Some churches we have consulted with have used crosses of thorn and thicket or of raw, unfinished wood. The semiotic is the stark brutality of a naked cross (which figureless can be intuited as our own false self). The light of tapers symbolizes the illumination of divine union.

almost presiderless service by having someone—most often Rector David Miller—vested in a simple black cassock and sitting in a simple chair in the center aisle. Sometimes two people so vested—a lay and an ordained person—sit in the transept on either side of the center aisle.

Order of Service

Opening Hymn: Solemnity and awe is the key here. We use a first-century pentatonic tune which Tom learned at Solesmes, with the text, "O Trinity of Blessed Light . . ."

Collect: ("Seek him who made the Pleiades . . ." Amos 5:8) is read slowly by our "nonpresiding" facilitator. The service slips back into silence for a moment's internalization of the reading.

A *Taizé chant:* We choose a chant that helps people with the centering—moving inward—process. "*Veni, Sancte, Spiritus*" is ideal because with only three words it is both centering and invocatory.

Silent, private practice of lectio divina: This is an experience of *lectio* as a personal, rather than shared discussion practice. A scripture passage[2] is read three times with three to four minutes of silence after each reading. The facilitator or even a designated lay member of the congregation can read this. (It would be preferable to read the passage only once, and then let people read it from the program. However, reading the passage aloud provides some sense of structure to the new participants.)[3]

Intercessory Taizé chant: Arising from the experience of silent prayer, intercessory prayer flows from the heart of people's concerns. We alternate sung and spoken intercession with the chant

---

2. Our favorite is John—the final discourse where the concept of a personal indwelling of God is so fully developed. Whatever the passage, it should be short enough to read in less than one minute. Our sense is to avoid theologically complex or charged passages.

3. At this point, those with a practice of Centering Prayer will generally close their eyes and internalize the Scripture. Those who do not have a contemplative prayer practice often follow the example. Brief program notes explain the prayer exercise for those who are new.

"*Adoramus Te,*" with intercessions spoken over a vocal organum drone between verses and refrain.

Adoration of the cross: Four to six Taizé chants are required to cover this extended period. The chants should be devotional and perhaps have solemnity. "Jesus, Remember Me" and "*Ubi Caritas*" are both exemplars and standards. The participants take their yet unlighted tapers and walk into the chancel, to a side of the sandbox, and kneel before the cross. They light their taper and place it in the sandbox. They then sit, kneel or stand around the cross, without a time limit.[4] We always have "ringers" ready to go up first, encouraging others, but never have the "ringers" proven necessary, as participants seem to rush the chancel. These volunteers however are useful in modeling sitting, kneeling, being around the cross, and in so doing, give everyone permission to do so.

Free will offering: This can be an apogee for those who believe the stewardship of financial giving should flow from an experience of God's presence. (We won't disclose collection figures, but often the per capita contribution is higher than the Sunday morning plate.)

Distribution of new tapers: We splurge and offer more tapers, distributed by volunteers walking just behind the ushers with the collection plate.

Concluding prayer: We generally use St. Augustine's "Late have I loved you, oh Beauty so old and yet so new. . . ." This again is read by one of the facilitators.

Taizé chant and lighting of congregational candles: We like to conclude with a boisterous, rousing, "jump up and shout" chant. "Sing Praise and Bless the Lord" is often used. As the song begins, adolescent volunteers take fire from the cross and bring it to the congregation.

Closure. We lower the lights. The sea of burning tapers lights the entire church and the tapers in the sandbox illuminate the bare cross. It is perhaps the most dramatic point of the service, with many disappointed the service is concluding. The facilitators

---

4. It is good to have cushions, chairs, and *prie-dieu* available.

remain in their seats to indicate that people can remain in the church. We leave it to each individual to decide when to extinguish the taper and when to leave the church. The carryover of the silent presence is always palpable. The facilitators and the musicians are encouraged to absent themselves in a manner that will discourage conversation.

The service takes one and a half-hours, including the thirty-minute period of Centering Prayer. If the Centering Prayer starts at 7:00, we are usually finished no later than 8:45.

Initially, the "adoration of the cross" was our biggest worry. We were so concerned that everyone would be too shy to participate. Before our "ringers" could get there, a flood of people were moving to the cross. The deep contemplative experience of the word had drawn people close to Christ's spirit within them and common inhibitions were cast off. Moments later the glow from the lighted tapers illumined a crowd kneeling and sitting at the foot of the cross, even kissing it (at St. Matthew's?), with others reaching past them just to touch the charred wood. The chancel was packed with people bowed in devotion, tears, healing and praise.

As we traveled around the country consulting with churches and parishes, conducting this new form of Taizé service, we always encountered some small, enlightening moment during the adoration of the cross. In Providence, Rhode Island, a group of adults with severe special needs formed a protective circle around the cross, singing in a language each his or her own, a joyous thunder which seemed to prove that God does not need the learned and the mighty to manifest great glory. Their leader was the last to leave this fire of Christ, dancing and waving a "V" for victory sign that left most of the congregation in tears. In a Washington, D.C., parish, situated between Embassy Row and the gay and lesbian community, the adoration of the cross was an occasion for numerous open vocal prayers, to loved ones lost to AIDS, with notes and letters placed at the foot of the cross and later consumed in its holy light. Many went back to pews but returned to the cross several times, celebrating what they said was for them a tangible experience of the communion of saints. In Santa Barbara, at the conclusion of the adoration, five young girls in white dresses danced into the chancel seemingly from nowhere (we hadn't noticed them earlier). They made up their own ritual, reciting spontaneous prayer, dancing around the cross, singing songs, and rearranging candles, which gave some of the altar guild adults a worry or two.

The message to us in these manifestations was to let the adoration run as long as the participant's movement of spirit wishes to express itself.

These experiences were not without some very humorous moments. The second outing at St. Matthew's was attended by double the expected crowd, about two hundred and fifty people. We didn't realize it, but our sandbox was too small and there were too many candles burning in too confined a space. There was a spontaneous combustion of the candles into a raging fire with flames licking five feet in the air. This burning symbol — fire dancing before the cross—was mesmerizing to most participants, who thought it was a planned element in an already dramatic service. We knew otherwise and had visions of St. Matthew's Church burning a second time. While Tom's dark side urged him to break into "Light My Fire" on the synthesizer, David and Gus devoutly exited the church and once outside, scrambled wildly to the sacristy, ransacking it for whatever textiles they could douse with water. With an air of forced composure they reentered the church with armloads of wet towels and cloths and knelt before the cross, gracefully extinguishing what was then a conflagration. Afterwards, many participants thanked us for the most moving and dramatic liturgical service they had ever attended. We three spent the next several hours removing candle wax from the saltillo tile floor before the good ladies of the altar guild discovered any stains. Though the sandbox was charred and beautifully complemented the burnt cross, the next service was supplied with a much bigger box and someone to monitor the flames.

The dynamic of this service, the blending of the profound silence of contemplative prayer with active prayer, mightily raises spiritual energies. Singing the chant seems to move these energies throughout the body and to settle them within our whole being. This prepares us for the experience of praying the Scriptures which effortlessly becomes a true "resting in God." Intercessory prayer, arising from this experience of Divine Indwelling, often summons in us the sense of being in creative partnership with God's healing powers. The movement of walking to the cross to kneel, sit, or stand gives physical, incarnational sense to the most subtle of spiritual experiences. The chant singing around the cross holds all in a spiritual and musical unity. Then, back in the pews, as people light more candles, the final, exuberant chant becomes a proclaiming shout. At the closure, many will not leave the church for another half-hour, not wanting to move beyond the strong, sacred environment. It is a an especially holy time for particular, personal prayer.

This form of Taizé is especially poignant the night before an introductory workshop on Centering Prayer. It establishes an experience of silent prayer in a Christian, scriptural context as being normative. It obviates any concerns or complaints that Centering Prayer is novel or inventive; indeed it places this ancient approach to contemplative prayer within the mainstream of the Christian contemplative heritage.

6

Systems Theory and Centering Prayer

PAUL LAWSON

> I do not understand my own actions. For I do not do what I want, but I do the very thing I hate. (Rom. 7:15)

When I returned from summer vacation, there was a call waiting for me from the minister of the church next to mine. I called him back. He told me that he had resigned from his church and he was going to retire from the ministry. Now, fifteen years later, I can't remember what the issue was. In general, the church governing board wanted him to ask their permission to do something he felt was his prerogative. In fact, this was not new, but a common occurrence with this board. He said that he had tried to call me and another minister. We had both been gone on vacation. So he resigned.

In talking with this minister, it seemed there was no particular reason he resigned from his church that evening. Nothing new had happened. He had just "had enough." Over the next several years, I noticed more and more similar cases in which the minister resigned because he had had enough. I also heard of several cases where the minister was fired because the congregation had had enough. Enough what? I wanted to know. Sometimes I asked. The reply was pretty much always the same: "Just enough," they said.

In some of these cases, there was not an apparent cause; in others there seemed to be many causes. Often, the clergy blamed the laity and the laity blamed the clergy. The diocese or church administrative body usually chose a side, and set about the task of replacing the clergy or silencing the laity. In many cases, this strategy was not successful. The problems in the congregations continued for years and, in some cases, for generations. There was one church I knew of that had gone from over 1500 members to less than fifty in twenty-three years. Other churches, I found, had had four pastors in five years. Churches developed reputations as being "clergy killers." Clergy developed reputations as being "problems."

By the time I joined a diocesan staff, I was convinced that an incident-based understanding of church conflict was not adequate and certainly not successful. The publication of Dr. Edwin Friedman's book, *Generation to Generation,* seemed to offer an alternative to a single event or single incident theory of church problems and conflict. Drawing on the works of Dr. Murray Bowen with the treatment of family groups with a schizophrenic member, which were later used in marriage and family therapy, Friedman proposed that congregations operate as a family system.

In examining family relationships, Bowen wrote,

> The total fabric of society, as it pertains to human illness, dysfunction, and misbehavior, is organized around the concept of man as an autonomous individual who controls his own destiny. When the observing lens is opened to include the entire family field, there is increasing evidence that man is not as separate from his family, from those about him, and from his multi- generational past as he has fancied himself to be.[1]

1. Murray Bowen, *Family Therapy in Clinical Practice* (Northvale, N.J.: Jason Aronson, 1994), 289.

Friedman took this understanding of family process and applied it to churches and synagogues. Friedman writes, "Everything that has been said thus far about emotional process in personal families is equally applicable to emotional process in churches, synagogues, rectories (which function as nuclear systems), and hierarchies (which function as extended systems). These too are families."[2] Friedman goes on to say that not only are churches families, but their members have families. This intensifies and complicates the emotional process. There is family process laid over family process.

Family interaction and process naturally produce anxiety.[3] The family and its members develop ways to absorb and bind this anxiety. Adaptations are made within the family structure. This process was created as part of our evolutionary heritage and can also be viewed in other life forms. But the anxiety produced in in the balancing of our relationships can also produce problems. Anxiety problems are seen in family systems in which there is a member of the family who is schizophrenic or a member who "causes trouble." In institutions, these same symptoms can be observed as problem individuals or problem events: "This clergy person is a real loser," or "This art show demeans our church and our God." Rather than deal with the individual symptoms or events or people, it may be better to deal with the underlying cause.

Dr. Daniel V. Papero, in writing about organizations and institutions, suggests that instead of focusing on individuals and their habits, a more profitable approach might be to focus on the functioning of the organization itself. In examining that functioning, one will find that a basic underlying variable in all organizations, is anxiety.[4] Within the organization anxiety effects not only individuals, but also the organization itself. Dr. Papero goes

---

2. Edwin Freedman, *Generation to Generation* (New York: The Guilford Press, 1985), 195.

3. Michael E. Kerr and Murray Bowen, *Family Evaluation* (New York: W.W. Norton & Company, 1988), 80.

4. Daniel V. Papero, "Anxiety and Organizations." In *The Emotional Side of Organizations: Applications of Bowen Theory*, ed. Patricia A. Comella (Washington: Georgetown Family Center, 01995), 47.

on to say that anxiety is more than just a psychological state; it actually describes the condition of the individual or organization.[5] In an individual or organization, anxiety has a marked effect on the ability to function. Intensified anxiety can produce heightened sensitivity to others, shifts in perception, changes in the way events are interpreted, and an increase in behavior that is automatic rather than thought-based.[6]

The concept of a church as an emotional system which produces anxiety in the natural course of its relationships, helps explain events, symptoms, and behaviors that surface in individual religious organizations. This understanding helps to explain what at times appear to be inexplicable courses of action taken by the leaders and membership of these organizations. Identifying and understanding the problem is only the first step. Time and energy can be saved by no longer engaging in unsuccessful programs for change that focus on the individual. There are no quick fixes or parts to be replaced. Instead, the relationships within the system need to be addressed in such a way that anxiety and frustration can be constructively managed and adjusted.

Centering Prayer

ONCE UPON A time there was a large and wealthy church in a sylvan setting. It looked peaceful, a place of worship and rest. The new minister lasted less than two weeks. It was believed that the minister received a six-figure settlement to leave and both sides considered it money well spent. It was thirteen days from the joy of a new arrival and ministry to uncivil war, acrimony, and recriminations. It was the Church in the latter part of the twentieth century.

The minister came to the new pastorate with high hopes. The congregation shared these hopes. The minister who had left had been at the church a long time, but in recent years had been waiting for his retirement. The new minister was coming to get things going again. There had been a long and careful search process looking for just the right person. When the new minister

5. Ibid., 47–48.
6. Ibid., 49.

arrived, he found several areas of the church, including an auxiliary organization, that were not under his direct control. When he tried to consolidate the different groups under his leadership, he met with resistance, then hostility, then opposition. He refused to back down because to do so would have been defeat. Besides, all areas of the church should be under his control. He had the right to make changes. Many in the congregation felt things were fine the way they were. After all, they had been like that for years. What right did the new minister have to make substantial changes so quickly? He was endangering the very fabric of the church. If he continued, there would be no church left. Who did he think he was anyway? Meetings were held. Secret meetings were held. Both sides got lawyers. Within two weeks the congregation was looking for a new pastor. How did things go so bad so quickly? How did the situation escalate so fast? Why was the end so violent? Emotions had gotten quickly out of control. The issues themselves were lost in what became verbal violence and confrontation. The battle became one for power, control, and esteem.

Various mediators who came into this situation began their work with a prayer or a prayer service. Visible effects of these oral prayers were not immediately evident. Perhaps a different method of prayer would have been more effective. *The Book of Common Prayer* of the Episcopal Church teaches about the kinds of prayer in the section "Catechism."

Q. "What is Prayer"

A. "Prayer is responding to God, by thought and by deeds, with or without words."

Church structures and organizations are, by their nature, rife with anxiety. Systems theory provides us with a way of understanding the processes at work within the congregation. But understanding congregational process and the anxiety that this process produces is not always enough. Many times we know how to act, we just don't seem to be able to act the way we desire. A prayer without words, Centering Prayer, provides us with an additional and complementary way of understanding what is happening in the church and also an effective way of working with the anxiety and emotions that are found within a congregation. Centering Prayer has the added benefit of having been taught in the church for over a thousand years. This makes it more accessible to church workers and leaders than natural systems theory. The combination of Centering Prayer and natural systems theory, when used together as complements, provide an effective model of church leadership and an effective avenue for congregational change.

Church writers and theologians have understood from the early centuries of Christianity that anxiety blocks relationship both with God and with human beings. Early writers such as Origen and Clement wrote about anxiety and emotions. Other early writers like Evagrius Ponticus and John Cassian offered practical solutions and courses of action. The solution that they offered to this situation of anxiety and emotion is *apatheia,* or the calming of passions which is achieved through silent prayer.

Modern writers such as Thomas Keating and Basil Pennington continue to write on this theme in modern language for current times.

In his book *Invitation to Love,* Father Keating describes how our relationships with others are often governed by emotional processes or programs that begin with our relations with our parents in infancy. Most people, says Keating, are unaware that these programs are functioning and influencing their behavior and judgments.[7] These programs set off emotional responses and reactions. Soon, before we are actually consciously aware of the situation, a difference of opinion has escalated into a full-scale emotional conflict. Sides are taken, lines are drawn in the sand, and there is no turning back or backing down. Relationships are strained and broken.

Relationship and Process

CENTERING PRAYER IS a prayer that is concerned with relationship: a person's relationship with God. As this relationship is strengthened

7. Thomas Keating, *Invitation to Love: The Way of Christian Contemplation* (Rockport Mass: Element Press, 1992), 8.

through Centering Prayer, so also are one's relations with other people. Keating calls this process, "Divine Therapy."[8] While the primary relationship that is addressed through Centering Prayer is with God, a side effect appears to be a healing of relationships with others. Centering Prayer and natural systems theory share several understandings and view the world in similar ways.

> Jesus said, "The first commandment is this: Hear O Israel The Lord our God is the only Lord. Love the Lord your God with all your heart, with all your soul, with all your mind, and with all your strength. The second is this: Love your neighbor as yourself. There is no other commandment greater than these." Mark 12:29–31[9]

One of the understandings that Centering Prayer and natural systems theory share is the importance of relationships. No individual person or event exists alone or lives or exists on an emotional island. In Christianity the importance of relationship is symbolized by the understanding of God as Trinity. Hans Kung writes that in considering the Trinity we must reflect on the relationship between God and Jesus with reference to the Spirit. He also writes about Father, Son, and Holy Spirit as a unity of operation and revelation.[10] God is in relationship with God's self and, through creation, calls humankind to be in relationship with God. The fall and salvation can be seen in terms of human beings attempting to sever their relationships with God, and God calling them back into relationship with God. In our estrangement from God we, as humans, also end up estranged from our neighbor.

> You made us . . . and we turned against you . . .
> and we turned against one another.
> Again and Again you called us to return.[11]

---

8. Thomas Keating, *Intimacy with God,* (New York: Crossroads, 1995), 72–75.

9. *The Book of Common Prayer* (New York: Church Hymnal Corporation, 1979), 351.

10. Hans Kung, *On Being a Christian* (Garden City, New York: Doubleday & Company, 1974) 75–77.

11. *Book of Common Prayer,* 370.

Centering Prayer and natural systems theory both place primacy on relationship. Sarah Butler writes, " . . . the practice of Centering Prayer is a common call to relationship."[12] Relationship with God, like relationships with other people, begins with dialogue. With God, sometimes our dialogue is formal and corporate, such as that which is found in our liturgy; at other times, it is personal and private. *The Book of Common Prayer* lists seven kinds of prayer: adoration, praise, thanksgiving, penitence, oblation, intercession, and petition. In some ways these are like our topics of conversation with other people. As relationships deepen, there comes a point when words are not necessary and just being in relationship with the other is enough; so too it is with God, and Centering Prayer provides a way to be in relationship through opening ourselves up to God's communication with us. Thomas Keating writes, "In time we will grow from a reflective relationship with God to one of communion. The latter is a being-to-being, presence-to-presence relationship, which is the knowledge of God in pure faith."[13] Centering Prayer is a way of being in relationship with God. The fruits of Centering Prayer are being in relationship with human beings. All of God's Creation is relationship and is in relationship.

Systems theory also sees the interconnectedness of the world. Peter Steinke writes, "Systems thinking is basically a way of thinking about life as all of a piece. It is a way of thinking about how the whole is arranged, how its parts interact, and how the relationships between the parts produce something new."[14] Natural systems theory begins with the understanding that all life is interconnected. Drawing on the work of E. O. Wilson in the field of sociobiology, systems theorists believe that relationship patterns and behaviors are common to all life. Murray Bowen made two major breaks with the thinking of the

---

12. Sarah Butler, "Pastoral Care and Centering Prayer," *Sewanee Theological Review,* Christmas 1996, Vol. 40:1, 58. (Also included in this volume, pp. 83–91.)

13. Keating, *Invitation to Love,* 87.

14. Steinke, *Healthy Congregations,* 3.

psychiatric community. The first was that the emotional functioning of humans was not particular to humans, but part of behavior patterns found in all animal life. To separate animal and human behaviors in functioning was to create an artificial dichotomy and to engage in intellectual constructs whose validity rested only in the human mind. Bowen's second discovery was that any understanding of human behavior must take into account the relationship system. In short, "Bowen proposed that the family operated in ways that were consistent with its being a system and that the system's principles of operation were rooted in nature."[15] Bowen himself extended this understanding of humans to groupings outside the family system, including work and social organizations. In describing these relationships, natural systems theory uses terms such as triangles, self-differentiation, family emotional systems, projection process, and multiple generation transmission process, all as ways of viewing and understanding human relationships. No person or functioning can be considered on its own, but only in the context of relationships both past and present.

The second area of similarity between Centering Prayer and natural systems theory is in the understanding of process. Much of Western thinking has been informed by the concept of history as shaped by single great individual or a single important event. A single person, taking a single action and single-handedly effecting change. This mechanistic model was taken from the physical world. If one exerts force on an object, it moves until the energy transmitted dissipates. People are different from physical objects in that they interact more, and are influenced by other people and the world around them. Within organizations, there have been traditionally two ways of looking at problem situations: One way has been looking at problem people; the other has been looking at problem events.[16] In the problem people approach, a problem can be solved only if the difficult person is changed or

15. Kerr and Bowen, *Family Evaluation,* 24.

16. George Parsons and Speed B. Leas, *Understanding Your Congregation as a System,* (Washington: Alban Institute, 1993), 4–5.

removed. In the problem event approach there is a specific problem to be solved and if everyone gets together it can be solved with a particular plan of action. Many management schools and consultants favor this approach and seek to put a problem-solving program in place. Both Centering Prayer and natural systems theory take a different approach. Understanding comes from thinking about and working with a whole process, not just a single person or event.

Christian mystic tradition has long considered a person's relationship with God to be not a static thing but rather a process. First, there is the process of the life journey. Athanasius's *Life of Antony* provides a look at that process. In the first step, Antony wants to be converted. He gives up his current life style; then, exhausted from the change, he turns to Christ. He does good works and finally in some sense becomes Christ. This process is called *theopoiesis* or being made divine.[17] Second, within Centering Prayer there is the process of the prayer itself and the effect that the prayer has on the individual. Father Keating writes about our relationship with God as being a developmental process. In a chapter about *lectio divina,* or the reading of the Scriptures, Keating draws on the medieval monastic understanding of the "four senses of Scripture"[18] That is, there are four levels of reading the Scripture: literal, moral, allegorical, and unitive. When the Scripture is read for the literal sense, it is read to find out what is happening and who is involved. When the same passage is read in the moral sense it is read for values and ways of behaving. In the allegorical sense, the passages are read to develop a life of practice for the reader. When the passages are read in the unitive sense, no action is required; rather there is a sense of resting in God, a oneness between God and the reader. During this reading process, a relationship is being developed with God. In the first stage, there is an acquaintanceship with God; in the second, there is more friendliness; in the third, a friendship

---

17. William A. Clebsch, preface to *The Life of Antony* by Athanasius (New York: Paulist Press, 1980), xvi.

18. Keating, *Intimacy with God,* 46.

develops; and finally there is union of life.[19] Centering Prayer is a process of interior transformation. This process of drawing closer to God and learning through unknowing is the subject of a poem by St. John of the Cross, *"Entreme donde no supe":*

> I came into the unknown
> and stayed there unknowing,
> rising above all science.
>
> I did not know the door
> but when I found the way,
> unknowing where I was,
> I learned enormous things,
> but what I felt I cannot say,
> for I remained unknowing,
> rising beyond all science.[20]

Natural systems theory is also based on and works through process. In defining process, Michael Kerr says that process is a continuous series of actions that result in a given set of circumstances or phenomena. Content, he writes, is taking those results out of the context of those actions. Edwin Friedman applies this understanding of "process" and "content" and specifically applies it to churches and congregations. Friedman writes, ". . . efforts to bring about change by dealing only with symptoms (content), rather than process, never will achieve lasting changes in an organic system."[21] The distinction that is drawn here is important for congregational change. Just as process is important for individual change through Centering Prayer, so too is it important in focusing on change in the congregation. Process is emotional and is about relationships. Content is about specific events and is usually a symptom of a problem in a relationship. What that means is if you solve one content problem, another content

---

19. Centering Prayer Contemplative Service Resources, Contemplative Outreach of Southern California Los Angeles, California. 1996, 8–9.

20. John of the Cross, "I came into the unknown," in *The Poems of John of the Cross*, trans. Willis Barnstone (New York: New Directions Book, 1972).

21. Friedman, *Generation to Generation*, 202.

problem will arise to replace it until the underlying process or relationship issues are addressed.

A bishop in the Episcopal Church used to ask his congregational leaders, Why is it that one priest could move altar candlesticks an inch and be fired, and another priest could move the church building across town and be given a raise? The answer to that question was that the issue was not about buildings or candlesticks, but rather was about relationship systems within the congregation. There are always content issues in a congregation; they can be about budget, theology, minister, members, guilds, or groups. Unless the relationship process is the focus, the content will continue to revolve from issue to issue.

The Role of the Emotions, Family of Origin, and Automatic Functioning

THE IMPACT OF the emotions on human functioning, the role of the family of origin in the development and response of these emotions, and the impact of these emotions on a person's ability to function are important concepts in both Centering Prayer and natural systems theory. Both Centering Prayer and natural systems theory see human emotions as a natural part of human existence, but a part of human existence which can easily dominate human behavior and lead to a reduction in thought-based decisions and a concomitant increase in automatic emotional functioning.

Emotions: Among the modern writers on the subject of prayer, Thomas Keating has the most developed understanding of the role the emotions play in a person's spiritual development. Keating writes, "Emotions faithfully respond to what our value system is."[22] Because of that, emotions are our best friends along the spiritual journey. While we can lie to ourselves about what is important to us, the emotions faithfully record what our true values are. Whenever our conscious or unconscious desires are

---

22. Keating, *Invitation to Love,* 19.

frustrated, our emotional response begins without any thought on our part. With each emotion there is a running commentary of wrongs done to us in the past, and those wrongs that might be done to us in the future. This commentary heightens a person's feelings and intensifies a person's response. This interaction between emotions and commentary is a process that is very hard to stop and often controls the way a person functions.

In natural systems theory, unlike Centering Prayer, emotions are not thought of as a description of a feeling or state such as anger, apathy or lust; rather they refer to a subjective experience of the emotional system. In a family, it describes the relationships among father, mother, and children; in an organization it describes the relationship among the members of that organization. "Emotional refers to all the systems that guide an individual automatically within an environment. These are instinctual behaviors that guide an individual."[23] These behaviors may include, but not be limited to, facial expressions and feelings—like falling in love, illness, migration, sex. The emotional system is shaped by the person and the person is shaped by the system.

The family and emotion: Centering Prayer and natural systems theory both see the family of origin as having a primary role in the emotional process. The relationship the person has within his or her family continues on throughout life. The way that a person functions within that family of origin is the way that he or she will continue to function throughout life.

Father Thomas Keating, writing about this process, describes it as emotional programs for happiness.[24] As infants, we have various wants and desires that remain unmet. Infants are, by nature, helpless, and their needs, both material and emotional, are met by others, often their parents or siblings. The primary caregiver holds, kisses, and hugs the infant, communicating love and affection. This gives the infant a feeling of security. But there is always a time in even the most cherished infant's life when the

23. Kathleen Dale MFCC, interviewed by author, 11 Dec. 1996.
24. Keating, *Invitation to Love*, 5.

primary caregiver is not available. As the infant becomes a toddler, she or he begins to compete with other family members for the time and recognition of the primary caregivers.

When the child moves out into the wider community, there is more competition, and often the child is frustrated satisfying basic needs. Later in life, we may not remember the actual events, but the emotional results of these events remain with us. For children who have suffered emotional trauma in the early part of their lives, the effects on the later part of their lives are that much more dramatic. The children may mature intellectually and physically, but emotionally they still react in ways that were developed in infancy.

We have an unlimited capacity for more: more power, more control, more affection, and more esteem. Within each of us, says Keating, there are emotional energy centers in which reside desires for these factors. The rejections, from our childhoods, both real and imagined, are carried forward into the present. These are not rational centers and don't require thought; they are emotional reactions on the subconscious level. Try as we might, we are unable to control them. So, instead, we replay our childhood reactions in our adulthood with disasterous results. This set of reactions becomes emotional programs for happiness that can't work because we are no longer children and we, as adults, can't meet those needs for power, control, affection, and esteem that we had as children.

A child, for example, may have never been chosen first to be on an athletic team on the playground. In fact, this child may have always been chosen last. As a result, as an adult he or she always strives to be chosen. Such people don't really want the job, the award, the spouse, they want to be chosen. When not chosen, they react with anger or sadness. These unconscious emotional programs for happiness are visible on the conscious level. They were catalogued as early as the fourth century, by Evagrius Ponticus, as gluttony, impurity, avarice, sadness, anger, restlessness, vainglory or pride.[25] These drives and desires,

---

25. Evagrius Ponticus, *The Praktikos,* trans. John Bamberger (Kalamazoo Mich.: Cistercian Publications, 1981), 6–14.

when in place, often cause us to function automatically, without thought and in response to relationships that we had in our family of origin.

Murray Bowen writes that the molecule of the family system is the triangle. The triangle is the smallest stable relationship system and the triangle has relationship patterns that repeat in times of stress. The original triangle is father, mother, and child.[26] The way a child functions, the role the child plays, the child's position in the family of origin is often the way the child will function later in life. Michael Kerr writes that, "The existence of a family emotional field is the product of an emotionally driven relationship process that is present in all families. . . . This emotional process results in people occupying different functioning positions in the family. A person's functioning position has a significant influence on his beliefs, values, attitudes, feelings and behavior."[27] This process of transmission of role, function and behaviors is not only generational but multigenerational. This is more than the past influencing the present, it is the past being present in the present. The result of all of this is that people are less free to make thoughtful decisions than might be supposed.

The automatic process: Centering Prayer and natural systems theory apologists see much of human functioning as unconscious and programmed. The area in our lives in which we make thought-based decisions is relatively small. Instead, we are driven by forces and processes outside our selves. Early Christian mystics such as Evagrius Ponticus described these as "demons" and wrote in terms of "temptations." This was language that was appropriate to its time in describing the human internal process. Modern Christian writers speak in terms of programs for happiness developed in childhood that are carried into adulthood. These programs represent values that, while they may be appropriate for a two-year-old struggling with life, are not appropriate for an adult. These values are represented by uncontrolled desires

26. Bowen, *Family Therapy,* 198–201.
27. Kerr and Bowen, *Family Evaluation,* 55.

for more affection, power, control, and esteem. This, in some sense, is the nature of sin. The emotions that these Christian writers describe are more limited in scope than the emotional processes that the systems theorists describe. The natural systems theorists would call "feelings" what the Christian writers describe as "emotions." The systems theorist's emotional field or system is a much broader concept, including not only feelings, but also other biological functions and processes.

Anxiety, say natural systems theorists, leads people to respond automatically to a perceived threat. The response may be based on the emotions, not on the reality of the threat. People who are more differentiated from the emotional systems around them will be aware of their own emotions and their response to the threat. The less differentiated person is more likely to react automatically in ways which are not appropriate to the reality of the threat.[28]

In either case, the result is to limit rational decision-making and functioning. One of the goals for both the Centering Prayer practitioner and the natural systems theorist is to increase thought-based decisions and decrease automatic functioning through the limiting of emotional reactivity and the development of an independent self.

The Projection Process

MURRAY BOWEN WRITES that parents often project their problems onto a child. In a family, a single child may be the focus or it may be more than one child. This is a process that is universal to all families and its purpose is to lessen anxiety. In recent times this has been called "scapegoating." This process can also be found in congregations which single out a clergy or member as being the cause of all their problems. If the person is removed, then the system will find a replacement for the person removed and no overall change will take place. Thomas Keating also writes of projection. People

---

28. James E. Jones, "Chronic Anxiety, the Adrenocortical Response, and Differentiation," *Family Systems* 1, no.2 (Fall/Winter 1994): 127–41.

will project onto others the responsibility for their happiness or unhappiness. People will project onto God their own needs for control, affection, power, and esteem. But both Centering Prayer and natural systems theory place responsibility on the self and not on beings outside the self.

The self: In both Centering Prayer and natural systems theory, the concept of self plays a central role. The self, says Thomas Keating, is made in the likeness of God with the ability to love unconditionally, create, nurture, and strengthen as is appropriate to a being created in God's likeness. But humans develop a self that is, instead, made in its own likeness, one that is based on a person's needs for affection, esteem, power, and control. Keating calls this self a false self.[29] The false self is built up from our desires for material goods and success, sometimes at the expense of others. This gives us a sense of self based on what we have, what and who we control and what other people think and say about us. This can also include identification with other groups and organizations to the point that we believe our worth is bound with the goals and success of the group. Benignly it could be a sports team, football, or a school; less benignly the National Socialist Party or Nazism. The false self is the self that we set up that tells us we need to satisfy the energy centers through a program for happiness that involves acquiring symbols of worth. These symbols enhance our self image in our own eyes. "I am a worthy person because I have a new house or a big car," or "I feel good when the USC football team wins because that means I am a winner."

The true self is one that needs only to be in relationship with God and whose purpose is to love unconditionally. It is for this purpose that humankind was created.

The concept of differentiation of self is at the core of natural systems theory, writes Daniel V. Papero.[30] This refers to the amount of differentiation between intellectual and emotional functioning.[31] On one end are people who are dominated in their

29. Keating, *Intimacy With God*, 163.

30. Daniel V. Papero, *Bowen Family Systems Theory* (Boston: Allyn and Bacon, 1990), 45.

intellectual and emotional functioning by the automatic emotional process of the family system. These people are less flexible and less adaptable in times of stress. This leads to greater reactivity to anxiety. At the other end are people who can function intellectually more independently from the family system and in times of stress are more adaptable and less reactive to anxiety. This independence allows them rational choices.

Within natural systems theory there is the concept of pseudo-self. The self is made up of clearly defined beliefs, opinions, convictions, and principles.[32] This self is unchangeable. The pseudo-self is acquired, conforms to the environment, and is created by the emotional pressure of the group. The pseudo-self can borrow self from others to enhance its well-being. Joining groups and identifying with other people are ways for this process to take place. A person who is continually in the process of self-differentiating is more able to make rational thought-based decisions, and less likely to be swept up in the reactivity of the moment.

A key in both Centering Prayer and natural systems theory is that the individual is responsible for himself. In natural systems theory there is the understanding that you cannot change the behavior of others, but you can change your reaction to that behavior. By changing your own reaction, you then impact the system around you. The change in your reactions will necessitate change in the actions of others.

In Centering Prayer, one of the recognized fruits of the prayer is unconditional acceptance of others. Centering Prayer changes the life of the person who prays, enabling him to act in the present without regard to what Thomas Keating calls the afflictive emotions and the commentary that build these emotions to a fever pitch.

Both Centering Prayer and natural systems theory seek to nurture and bring out a self that can act freely and independently of the pressures within the systems of which they are a part. In both of these understandings, it is a life-long and continuing

31. Bowen, *Family Therapy,* 363.
32. Ibid., 365.

process rather than a thing achieved in a moment and possessed from that moment on. In both of these systems a person becomes a "true self" or a "differentiated self" through gaining the ability to act consciously and independently while still being connected to others through relationship.

Physiology: It has long been known that the body and mind act upon each other. A major theme in both theology and philosophy, beginning with the Greeks, has been the struggle between the mind and body. They have, at times, been portrayed as being at war with each other. The mind is generally given the role of controlling the desires of the body. The body is given the role of leading the mind astray along the path of concupiscence. Balance between the two needs to be maintained. Peter Brown writes, "An unaffected symbiosis of body and soul was the aim both of medicine and philosophical exhortation."[33]

Centering Prayer and natural systems theory both adhere to the understanding that there is a close relationship between the mind and the body. In the history of Christian mysticism, physiological effects have long been recorded. The histories of the Desert Fathers and Mothers and *The Life of Antony* all record physiological changes that take place during prayer. Evagrius Ponticus writes about the effects of anger on the body. Anger leads to indignation and "this is succeeded by a general debility of the body, malnutrition with its attendant pallor and the illusions of being attacked by poisonous wild beasts."[34] These effects need to be noted or observed and opposed with prayer. Evagrius writes ". . . when you grow angry . . . then is the time to put yourself in mind of prayer. . . .You will find that the disordered movement will immediately be stilled."[35] The author of *The Cloud of Unknowing* also writes of this relationship, ". . . for it is God's will to be served in both body and soul together as is seemly, and to

33. Peter Brown, *The Body and Society* (New York: Columbia University Press, 1988), 27.

34. Evagrius Ponticus, *The Praktikos,* 11.

35. Evagrius Ponticus, *Chapters on Prayer,* 12.

give man his reward, in bliss, both in body and soul."[36] The benefits of *apatheia* achieved in prayer stressed by the early Christian writers, from Clement to Cassian, provided not only mental relief from stress and anxiety but also physical relief.

The body–mind connection is also noted by writers of natural systems theory. Physiology is part of the greater relationship system, writes Louise Rauseo. In her article, "Relationships as Primary Regulators of Physiology," she maintains that social relationships and physiology are related and are important in understanding a person's life course. Heart rate, blood pressure, and other physical factors have long been known to be affected by the reactivity among people.[37] Disease is often found where there are troubled human relationships. Rauseo says, "Physiology is as sensitively tuned to the `charge' of important relationships as it is to external life-threatening dangers. Information about relationships is often pre-verbal and may bring about responses before a thought is formed."[38] Instability in the emotional or family system can lead to physical changes. These can include heart attack, asthma, colitis, and perhaps even depression and varicose veins. People with higher levels of differentiation are not as affected as those people who have lower levels of differentiation and are therefore more reactive to the relationship system.

If the natural systems theory understanding of physiology and its connection with the relationship system is valid and the Christian mystic's understanding of the effects of prayer is also correct, then it may be that Centering Prayer could be used as a way of counteracting the physiological symptoms of relationship. Prayer could be a method of directly moderating anxiety and its physical effects. Centering Prayer might be a way of lowering the overall reactivity of the relationship system in a congregation.

---

36. *The Cloud of Unknowing*. ed. James Walsh (Ramsey, N.J.: Paulist Press, 1981). Chap. XLVIII.

37. Louise Rauseo, "Relationships as Primary Regulators of Physiology," *Family Systems* 2, no. 2 (Fall\Winter 1995): 106.

38. Ibid., 113.

Implications for Congregational Leadership

THE FIRST IMPLICATION for leadership is that congregational systems need to be understood as mutuality or reciprocity. In this way of thinking, A does not cause B so much as A and B influence each other. In the congregation all the people who make up that body, lay and ordained, leader and follower, regular attender and occasional visitor, and their families and generations of families all mutually influence each other. Congregational leadership looks at the relationship that all these different people, parts, and events have with each other and how they function in relation as part of one another. Centering Prayer helps us to experience ourselves as part of the greater whole of God. It helps us to feel and to be in relationship with God and God's creation.

The second implication is that leadership is best achieved through the process of self-differentiation. The leaders need to take responsibility for themselves, their actions, and their responsibility in the system. Leaders need to define their own objectives and goals and work towards them while staying in touch with other parts of the congregation.[39] Most importantly staying in touch with those parts of the congregation that are opposed or working actively against the goals and objectives of the leader. The leader also needs to be as nonreactive as possible. The Centering Prayer goal of *apatheia* becomes a necessity in congregational leadership. This can only be achieved with an active Centering Prayer practice on the part of both lay and ordained leaders. Those leaders, in turn, need to be supported by active Centering Prayer groups within the congregation. Active Centering Prayer lowers the overall reactivity of both the individuals and the congregation as a whole. Centering Prayer also works to slow down or interrupt the physiological effects of increased reactivity and anxiety. Natural systems theory can help us understand the emotional field that is a congregation and the position of the leader in that system. But theory needs the compliment of Centering Prayer to effectively work within that system and maintain the nonreactive leadership position.

---

39. Friedman, *Generation to Generation*, 229.

The third implication is that everyone in the congregational system needs to observe their own behavior and position within the system and objectively see the ways that they function within the system. The more objective one is, the more able they are to see the role that they play in whatever the current issue is and not blame others. The answer to any question is always "me," because both Centering Prayer and natural systems theory both teach that the only person that one can affect is "me." Michael Kerr writes, "If one does not see himself as part of the system, his only options are either to try to get others to change or withdraw."[40] If, on the other hand, one accepts responsibility for one's position in the system and remains objective about the position one plays, then the amount of reactivity will decrease. The purgative process of Centering Prayer allows one to the act in the present in a more objective and less reactive manner.

The last implication for congregational leadership is that reactivity and anxiety can only be reduced in an open congregational system. Murray Bowen writes, "Relative openness does not increase the level of differentiation in a family, but it reduces anxiety, and a continued low level of anxiety permits motivated family members to begin slow steps toward better differentiation."[41] Centering Prayer begins a process of openness though its purgation of past hurts and an opening of a greater relationship with God. This experience of a loving relationship with God provides a model of being loved unconditionally. This personal experience of being loved unconditionally provides the example and the security one needs to love other people unconditionally. This, in turn, leads to a willingness to risk being open with others.

Centering Prayer and natural systems theory are companions in the process of congregational leadership. Centering Prayer makes possible the self-differentiation that natural systems theory requires. The personal healing of Centering Prayer leads to the possibility of congregational healing as the spiritual health of the individual, in a systems view, affects relationships throughout the whole system.

---

40. Kerr, *Family Evaluation*, 272.
41. Bowen, *Family Therapy*, 537.

7

Pastoral Care with Centering Prayer

SARAH A. BUTLER

As a canon for pastoral care in an urban cathedral, I have witnessed a great many lay people training for pastoral ministry who embrace the practice of Centering Prayer as a means of nurturing their own faith. I believe there is a subconscious attraction to Centering Prayer and *lectio divina* (from which it derives) because they share the fundamental elements and rhythms of effective pastoral care. Or perhaps it is because effective pastoral care mirrors the full range of prayer: from active and attentive modalities to resting in God's presence. In my ministry I identify these rhythms and elements as: the human/divine collaboration, care and prayer as relationship, and the parallel dynamics of *lectio divina* and pastoral care.

The Human/Divine Collaboration

MY EXPERIENCE HAS taught me that the most effective pastoral caregivers are those who humbly and consciously recognize that their ministry—from intention to effect—is a gift from God. However, even the most gifted caregivers among us can get so caught up in the activity and importance of our enterprise that we forget this larger view of our ministry. Indeed, it is easy to fall into the subtle seduction of doing too many good works on the power of our own talent and strength. I know I have fallen into this trap and have found myself talking to God in prayer as I would instruct an efficient secretary to organize my calendar, carry out my delegated requests, and act as a buffer for those annoying interruptions which thwart my ministry and my life. When I catch myself doing this, I try to remember what part of pastoral care is my responsibility and what part God directs.

Foolhardy as it may seem, I have written job descriptions for the caregiver and for God, a human/divine collaboration of sorts. Reading these whimsical job descriptions almost always jolts me back from feeling that the whole task rests with me or that I have a monopoly on God's services. They might be summarized as:

> *Care minister's job description:* The foremost responsibility is to be human and to respond to another person's suffering in humility, knowing that a caregiver can neither see the future nor be certain of what is best for the care-recipient. We can only consent to God's presence and action.
>
> *God's job description:* To be divine.

God does a far superior job of sticking to this plan than does the caregiver. When I find my ministry "off center," it is because I sometimes operate as if God were human and I were divine. I notice this most as a lack of joy and soon find myself in need of a moment of remembrance, a call to wonder, to see that it is God who initiates and we who respond.

In pastoral situations we always pray for God's intervention as though God were blissfully unaware of the crises and required our supplications. However, God is already active in the heart and life of both care-receiver and caregiver long before the faintest whisper of need and longing. Our prayers should not be an alarm for God's attention but a request to participate in God's healing process. Indeed, we function best as pastors when we recognize that we are a part of a process greater than our efforts, which is the healing that God has initiated. If we, like the Apostles, presume that feeding the five thousand rests on our shoulders alone, what hope do we have? However, like the lad in the Gospel story who humbly offers his little cache of five loaves and two fishes to Jesus to help feed five thousand, we are quickly relieved to see that all we can offer is just our presence and compassion. God does the rest, responding with the divine surprise, using our limited offerings to effect great works.

In Centering Prayer we are drawn into the same human/divine collaboration. The efficacy of prayer does not rest with us. It is God's initiative. We need only respond with consent to the presence and action of God within us. The practice of Centering Prayer calls for a silent receptivity, a "letting go" of control ("I'm divine"), or of notions about how God should respond (God as efficient secretary). This prayer of silence and letting go is a deep confirmation of our trust in the strength of the Lord. Do we believe that God is only capable of responding when we do the talking? Or does prayer also include a time of listening? In prayer, listening rather than talking or asking can be a surrender to the mystery and wisdom that our eyes, ears, and intellect cannot access (1 Cor. 2:7–10). Indeed, Centering Prayer is defined by its proponent Thomas Keating as a method that facilitates contemplative prayer, which he describes as:

> It is the opening of mind and heart. . . . Moved by God's sustaining grace, we open our awareness to God, who we know by faith is within us, closer than breathing, closer than thinking, closer than choosing—closer than consciousness itself.[1]

It is from this privileged place within us where the Spirit dwells, where we access and receive Holy Wisdom (Rom. 8: 26–27), that the Spirit flows outward through our gifts into the tangible world. The rhythms of Centering Prayer—from knowing to unknowing, from doing to being, from information to formation, from context to contemplation—renew the wonder and awe that keeps us ever mindful of God at the center of our lives, just as God is the center of the pastoral care relationship.

---

1. Thomas Keating, *Intimacy with God*, (New York: Crossroad, 1995), 41.

In our daily life this spiritual attentiveness of God's living presence can cause a fundamental shift in our self-identity—from knowing to unknowing, from the certainty of our needs to the infinity of pastoral needs to which God ministers. Analogously, over 450 years ago the universe was thought to revolve around the earth. Humankind, master of earth, was the center of creation. The Copernican discovery that the universe did not revolve around the earth caused a cataclysmic shift in human consciousness. Now science tells us that the universe, born of infinite energy, is still expanding and moving. Our earth-centered consciousness has given way to a vision of an infinite universe; similarly, our ego-centered personal consciousness can open to the infinity of union with the divine.

In Centering Prayer, as in the pastoral relationship, we may begin with our projections or with other gods such as superstitions, personal whims, or ignorance. All of these drain our spiritual energies. If we can listen and allow God's initiative to spark the fire of love, however, we can go beyond word, thought, and emotion—beyond verbal, mental, and affective prayer—to the awe of God without limits. Humility blossoms as we realize it will take an eternity to fathom the depths of God's love. Certainly, this is what Saint John of the Cross meant when he sighed that we are all beginners.[2] Indeed, the metaphor becomes reality as that humble posture of openness to God's unfolding presence reveals a place of unknowing where mystery and matter meet.

Care and Prayer as Relationship

A SECOND STRIKING parallel between pastoral care and the practice of Centering Prayer is a common call to relationship. Pastoral caregivers should quickly learn that they are not in the business of solving problems. They must learn instead to place emphasis on developing a caring relationship and becoming a supporting

---

2. See *The Collected Works of St. John of the Cross,* Kieran Kavanaugh and Otilio Rodriguez, trans. (Washington, D.C.: ICS Publications, 1991), vol. 2, chap. 12, "The Ascent of Mount Carmel."

presence. Though there may be many healing results from careful listening and respectful presence, expectations should always rest on offering up the outcome to God's love.

Pastoral care naturally begins in dialogue. An intimacy and comfort in the relationship develops that can embrace prayerful silence. Though this cannot be rushed, it can be nurtured by a full acceptance of the care-receiver's story. Such acceptance often is sensed as a permission to let go of anxiety and worry about the future and rest in the caregiver's presence as a witness to God's hope.

Like pastoral care, the relationship of prayer generally begins in dialogue. Whether we pray with the Scriptures or by speaking directly with God, we begin in an individual context as we express our needs of petition, intercession, penitence, and oblation. These expressions make possible the unfolding of our story and God's place in it. They are essential steps in the development of a full relationship with God. Many Christians, though, never go beyond these more active modalities of prayer. Many never enter into any regular practice of adoration "asking nothing but to enjoy God's presence."[3]

Corporate worship epitomizes the flow from context to contemplation, particularly in the celebration of Communion where matter meets mystery in the sacramental elements. In the Anglican tradition the simple term "real presence" is the favored definition of God's action in the Eucharist and our surrender to the mystery.

We must begin with prayer as the expression of our needs, but we must go further. We must allow such prayers to unfold themselves, to draw us out of our selves into the heart of faith where mere words cannot communicate. As the prayer of God's presence develops, we become less dependent on language and eventually surrender to the silent mystery of God's "real presence." The method of Centering Prayer enables the unfolding movement from the more verbal modes of prayer to the silence of contemplative prayer.

---

3. *The Book of Common Prayer* (New York: Church Hymnal Corp., 1979), 847.

Another ingredient vital to pastoral care and Centering Prayer is intention. Our intention to offer pastoral care is identical to our intention to be with God through Centering Prayer: *just being there.* This posture is humorously captured by comedian Woody Allen's statement: "Ninety six percent of success is just showing up."[4] How many prophets in the Old and New Testaments tried to refuse God's call with excuses, "I'm too old," "I'm too young," "Nobody will listen," or—even more terrifying—"What happens if they *do* listen?" God's response to almost every prophet's reticence, however, is, "Just show up. I'll do the rest; you'll be amazed at the results. You be human. I'll be divine."

Many pastors responding to crises—perhaps feeling exhausted or irritated at the time—have discovered with some amazement that it was their mere presence that served as the catalyst for bringing God's compassion and healing into a difficult situation. God somehow uses our willingness just to "show up," our humble part of the human/divine collaboration, as the yeast or lump of clay, the last ounce of oil and flour to make a miracle. Intention in pastoral care can sometimes be all, eclipsing even the best skill, training, and professionalism.

So, too, in Centering Prayer. Thomas Keating counsels that sometimes just sitting to pray, even when one is tired, distracted, or distraught, is the greatest act of intention. God responds above all to our *presence* and not to our *performance* in prayer.

> Centering Prayer . . . is an exercise of *intention.* It is our will, our faculty of choice, that we are cultivating. The will is also our faculty of spiritual love, which is primarily a choice. It may be accompanied by sentiments of love but does not require them. Divine love is not a feeling. It is a disposition or attitude of ongoing self-surrender and concern for others similar to the concern God has for us and every living thing.[5]

Centering Prayer does not depend on our moods, distractions, or fatigue; it does, however, rely upon our unrelenting

---

4. Woody Allen, *Annie Hall* (Farmington Hills, Mich.: CBS/FOX Video, 1985). Released as a motion picture by United Artists in 1977.

5. Keating, *Intimacy with God*, 57.

intention to be with God. We discover that even in sitting to begin our practice that we are more than the sum of our distractions. Centering Prayer bids us beyond the context of our thoughts (no matter how collected or frazzled), beyond our feelings (no matter how tranquil or distraught), beyond all selfish concerns into the contemplative dimension of naked, loving presence. The silence nurtures us mysteriously. We return to our daily lives restored, strengthened, and peaceful—not because we seek this in our prayers but because we only seek God and God seeks us. It is not the subjective experience in prayer, ranging from tranquility to incessant distraction, but our intention of consent to God's presence and action within us that transforms us.

C. S. Lewis in *The Screwtape Letters* casts this issue in a simple prose paradigm: Screwtape often advises Wormwood to teach his human to analyze the value of his prayers in terms of the feelings they produce and to judge the success of prayer as being wholly dependent on the human's state of being at the moment of prayer. His devilish advice was to keep all prayer subjective and to fix one's longing gaze on one's self rather than on God.[6]

The Parallel Dynamics of Lectio Divina and Pastoral Care

THE RHYTHMS OF *lectio divina* and effective pastoral care are strikingly clear. *Lectio divina* is the Christian contemplative tradition's way of reading anD praying with the Holy Scriptures. It leads one into deeper relationship and, ultimately, contemplative union with God. Distilled from *lectio divina,* the method of Centering Prayer attempts to facilitate the transition from the active modes of prayer, from mental and affective prayer *(meditatio* and *oratio),* to the silent, awe-filled prayer of presence *(contemplatio).* An established practice of Centering Prayer enriches the practice of *lectio divina.*

Lectio divina begins in reading and reflecting. From there it moves into a dialogue with God and our emotional responses. It eventually ends with our resting in the silence of divine presence.

---

6. C. S. Lewis, *The Screwtape Letters* (New York: Macmillan, 1961), 16, 20, and elsewhere.

This movement echoes the rhythms of pastoral care. Out of this "conversation," through which we learn the care receiver's story, emerges the intimacy that allows self-disclosure. The dynamic of intimacy and self-disclosure allows the caregiver to move into the peace where one can offer a quiet presence, the contemplative dimension of caregiving.

Another striking comparison between *lectio divina* and pastoral care is the value of the repetition of the story. One reading of scripture is simply inadequate to uncover the reflections and responses that can be elicited from the text. Likewise, the person who has undergone a crisis needs to be able to repeat the event over and over again. This repetition first allows what seemed impossible to begin to become real. As the story continues to be retold, nuances are noticed that will become part of one's sacred story. Healing takes place as both caregiver and care-receiver express multiple feelings, ask difficult questions, and listen to God's call to reorder that which was in disorder. In time, the need to know all the answers gives way to faith and an appreciation of God's sustaining grace.

Consider the following parallels between the dynamic of *lectio divina* and pastoral care:

Lectio Divina	Pastoral Care Ministry
Read the story in God's Word (lectio): Be present to the Word. Listen to the story for information.Take it in. Get acquainted with the passage scripture.	*Listen to care-receiver's story:* Be present to the person. Listen to story for information. Receive it nonjudgmentally. Get acquainted with the person.
Reflect (meditatio): Become actively involved with the story. *Pay attention to what attracts your attention.* Notice your own feelings. Reflect on your own inner experience of the scripture. Allow the Gospels to be a mirror of your own life.	*Reflect:* Focus on the feelings. *Pay attention to what attracts your attention.* Begin to see the unique person that God loves. Recognize and accept the person's inner experience. Mirror back your perception of the care-receiver's inner experience.

Respond (oratio): Be free to express what is pouring out of the reflection—praise, tears, repentance, thanksgiving. How is God becoming formed in you? Celebrate this with accepttance.

Rest (contemplatio): Let go of all reflections and responses in order to allow God to speak to you in the mystery of silence and quiet presence. Surrender to the mystery and awe.

Respond: Allow the person to respond to the mirroring above—with tears, possible insight, experience, repentance, thanksgiving. Celebrate this by encouraging acceptance

Rest: Let go of the need to know the outcome. Offer prayer, silence, or just your presence. This is the contemplative dimension of caring. Sit in awe of God's divine action in the other.

Life crises or painful events plunge us into the reality of our human frailty. They represent a ripe opportunity to offer our helplessness as the context in which God's healing grace can be initiated. When we are the most empty and confused, our greatest need is the presence of someone who cares. The caring priest or lay minister must not arrive armed with answers but with faith and the courage simply to be mindfully present to someone in pain. Similarly, we must not arrive in prayer with an agenda of wants, needs, and directives for how God should respond. Often, it is precisely because life crises underscore our inability to order and control our world that these events become turning points. The reordering process, or transformation, is an invitation to the discovery of divine surprise in all of life. Likewise, a regular practice of Centering Prayer also draws us into our deepest place of emptiness; it is an acknowledgment that we cannot completely control and order our lives, that we are wholly dependent on God. It is our consent that opens a space for God's reordering of our lives, that allows a transformation to take place.

All pastors, lay or clergy, can learn valuable skills and benefit immeasurably from mutual ministry support activities. Our experiences at the Cathedral of St. John in Denver have led us to make available not only pastoral care but also Centering Prayer and *lectio divina* as means of exploring the divine/human collaboration. This enables us to receive our ministry as a gift and as an invitation to share in Christ's larger ministry of divine union with us all.

8 ❋

Centering Prayer and Community

DAVID FORBES MORGAN

> In a Centering Prayer community, we become one not just with the people in the room and all those truly seeking God: we also become one with everything that God has created: with nature, with art, with relationship with the service of others. This bonding effect gives us an inner desire to form community and to be faithful to it, even if with only one other person.[1]

The experience of Centering Prayer came to me at an early age, when I was a child I worshiped with my parents in a faith community known as the Plymouth Brethren. Each Sunday we gathered for the principle Christian service of Holy Communion—word and sacrament which lasted approximately an hour and a half. There was an appreciation of silence and solitude which resulted in a service full of prayer in addition to Holy Scripture, hymns, and Holy Communion. During the service we experienced

---

1. Thomas Keating, *Intimacy with God* (New York: Crossroads Publishing, 1994), 158.

some twenty to thirty minutes of intermittent silence. In the silence, the gathered community of faithful Christians, in addition to traditional forms of prayer, was engaging in the prayer of adoration—prayer without words, concepts, or thoughts.

My father would often ask me how I was doing with the silence, and I would acknowledge that at times my mind drifted to thoughts about my friends, toys, and other childlike interests. He suggested that while those things were an important part of my life, they were not really the immediate purpose for which we were gathered as a community. He told me that when this happened I should simply return to the name of Jesus, gently forming it in my subconscious, allowing myself to rest in the Spirit. This practice brought me deeply into relationship with the divine presence. It further transformed me as I became deeply aware of my relationship to the people in the community and the course of their spiritual journey, which was an integral part of mine.

The goal of that faith community was interior purification leading to union with the divine. A further intention of this fellowship was deep appreciation of Holy Scripture. Listening to the word of God with the ears of the heart, pondering deeply its literal, allegorical, and spiritual meaning, led to resting in God's presence. It represented a unique encounter with Christ where thought and conversation became a confluent movement into communion with the divine presence. It was indeed a practice of *lectio divina,* the traditional way of cultivating friendship with Christ.

In subsequent years it has been easy to identify this early experience as one with the form of Centering Prayer developed by Abbot Thomas Keating and his fellow Cistercian monks, William Meninger and Basil Pennington, who were inspired by the fourteenth-century text, *The Cloud of Unknowing.* Through my personal association with them and subsequent visits to such ecumenical communities of Taizé in France, and the Communauté de Grandchamp in Switzerland, I percieved more clearly the three areas so common to monastic life: contemplative prayer, *lectio divina,* and vowed community life. In the context of Post-Vatican II, these three disciplines have leaped over monastic walls to become linchpins of the participation by the laity of the Church and its movement in deeply disciplined Christian living. They have also been instrumental in the formation of the Order of Christ Centered Ministries, the ecumenical community associated with the National Episcopal Church, of which I've been a part since 1973.

In all communions of the Christian Church, there is a desire for more intentional community. It is a movement of the Holy Spirit to ratify the intention of the divine forming prescence within, thereby making ministry truly caring and effective. The work of the body of Christ truly becomes one with divine purpose.

As Thomas Keating has written, "Contemplative prayer is part of a dynamic process that evolves through personal relationship rather than by strategy."[2] Community is the antidote to the desperate surge of individualism and its implied struggle to climb the ladders of success. The resultant loneliness of our time has rent assunder the process of relationship. Consequently, commitment to even the simplest of relationships is often suspect.

Dialog with others is important, but joyfully adoring the presence of God in the other, whether in strength or in weakness, is basic. Being present to each other even under the most trying circumstances gives God opportunity to work. Joy invariably comes after the night of frustration . . . when morning dawns with new light. Community deepens our intention not to let go of the divine possibilities in the other and in us.

We learn that we are not in the business of changing others. This is God's work! God's divine thrust and reception—the masculine and feminine components of new life nurtured in community

I am not suprised that wherever I find myself in ministry I am confronted with the deep desire of mind and heart for community and a sense of belonging. The loss of family ties and common goals that formerly fused people together has left a vacuum that only commitment to relationship rather than strategy can heal. Undoutedly, strategic planning has its place, but only a prayerful, listening community can effect true healing from brokenness and the promised rest of divine union. The call for commitment to community life comes from the mind and heart of a God who is in relationship expressed richly in the concept of the Holy Trinity.

---

2. Thomas Keating, *Open Mind, Open Heart* (New York: Continuum, 1992), 15.

The writer of the Letter to the Hebrews reminds us, "Only faith can guarantee the blessings that we hope for, or prove the existence of the realities that at present remain unseen."[3]

Community can be a safe place of belonging where one enters into a new dimension of relationship by listening more carefully to someone else allowing God's unconditional love to permeate all of life. Sharing, sitting, standing, walking, and kneeling with others means that eyes meet, hands touch, tasks are shared, and new light, life, and love mysteriously blend with commitment. The true self at one with God becomes increasingly evident, though sometimes elusive.

> A human response to God's call has many faces. Its nuances reflect joy and sorrow, hope and hurt, progress and failure, yet constant determination in commitment. The pain of knowing without being always challenges those dedicated to the realization of God's perfect will.[4]

Living in isolation we may be tempted to believe that we can love everyone. In the community, the demoniac thrusts of the wounded self are exposed as naked vulnerability blocking our progress to divine union.

We must never fail to realize that in the midst of the paradox of community, there will always be a desire to escape—to once more become a loner. Jesus' disciples bear testimony to the fact that when they chose to seperate from the apostolic community they were capable of expressing rejection, misunderstanding, denial, betrayal, and abandonment

The purpose of community then is to embrace a relationship which calls forth commitment of the mind and heart to prayer, to reading and listening to Holy Scripture *(lectio divina)*, and to sharing the call of God to minister to the poor and broken. In the awareness of our own brokenness and poverty of Spirit, we are guided in our spiritual journey to deepening friendship, increased light, new life, and the capacity to give and receive unconditional love. Loving unconditionally brings together the two roles of

---

3. Hebrews 11:1 (New Jerusalem Bible).

4. David Forbes Morgan, *Christ Centered Ministries, A Response to God's Call* (Denver: Christ Centered Publishers, 1973), 3.

community: a sense of belonging to each other and a desire that each person develops further in giftedness to God and to others.

Living and working together in community nurtures the mind and heart in truth and peace, enabling one to truly become a more caring minister of God's grace. It challenges one to live out of the center where God dwells.

The tradition of Christian community recognizes a call to the contemplative dimension of the gospel out of which action on behalf of all creation is manifested. At one with the mind and heart of Christ, the call to minister to broken, poor, and dispossessed persons becomes the focus of ministry.

Recognizing the value of commitment to prayer, reading and listening to Holy Scripture, and responding in community, let us examine the way in which these three avenues of discipline enable one to consent to transformation.

Contemplative Prayer (Employing the Centering Prayer method)	*Lectio Divina*	*Community*
Embrace the affirmation that the risen Jeus is among us as the glorified Christ living in each of us, present everywhere at all times. Formally begin the relationship of prayer by becoming acquainted.	*Lectio*—Read and listen to the story of God's grace with the ears of your heart. Become familiar with the information being given, seek to record it. Personally encounter Christ.	*Cooperate*—Be present and listen to those God has called you to be with. Let your heart embrace their strengths and woundedness with God's healing grace. Offer yourself to each one in weakness or in strength. Get acquainted.
Consent to God's presence and action within you and manifested everywhere and in everything. Recognize relationship with the divine presence in the context of friendly conversation	*Meditatio*—Ponder and reflect. Let Holy Scripture mirror your heart and unfolding life. Enter into discursive meditation.	*Consider*—See each person as important to you. Consent to the divine possibilities in your true self, one with God, and the true self in others. See no one as unimportant, as dispensable.

Permit the work of the Divine prescence within to take place, knowing that the unloading of the false self moves you to the expulsive power of a new awareness and affection. Do not fear: only trust in God's unconditional love. Enter into commited friendship.

Oratio—Respond to the work of God's Spirit. Acknowledge woundedness and recovery in Christ Jesus. Celebrate all creation and God's redeeming graces inwardly. Permit trust to be renewed. Praise God! Give thanks! Weep! Ask for forgiveness! rejoice! Be spontaneous!

Comfort—Console and enourage those who are suffering in their woundedness and the unloading of the false self. Be open to the vision of others. Speak kind words to everyone and celebrate their uniqueness. Seek to enable and encourage.

Open—Rest in the silence and solitude. Open by faith to the ultimate mystery, the rooted ground of your being and the source from whom life emerges. Let intimacy draw you into the union of life.

Contemplatio—Rest in silence and solitude. Let the supreme divine forming mystery possess your being—all that you are or hope to be. Surrender to the divine forming mystery. Be a mystic. Embrace the unknown with love.

Calm—Rest with a nonanxious presence regarding others. By faith, believe that God's grace is operating at all times. Remember peace is each step of the way.

An addendum to this reflection might be expressed by adding a new concept to *Lectio Divina–operatio*—a continuing discipline.

Remain in prayer.

Continue to read and prayerfully listen.

Perservere in community

After musing on these comparisons it might be helpful to recall the admonition of Evelyn Underhill.

> Look now at the aim which should condition your inner life. This aim . . . cannot and must not be that of becoming a contemplative pure and simple. It must rather be to transform your whole life of action and service with the spirit of poverty.[5]

5. Evelyn Underhill, *Considering the Inner Life* (Oxford: One World, 1995), 40.

The practice of Centering Prayer recognizes God's initiative in the relationship of prayer and calls for silent openness and receptivity. It slowly but surely enables one to "let go" of the inordinate need for control, the egotistical desire for self esteem and the anxiety relevant to personal security.

Involvement in Christian community empowers us to release preconceived ideas for personal solutions. It assists us in that we gradually recognize that we do not need to be the center of attention and labor indiscriminately to acquire a security package. It becomes a haven for knowing where inner life and outer care unite and meet to glorify God.

The fundamental disposition in Centering Prayer is one of opening to the Spirit. Christian life and practice can be summed up in the word *patience.* In the New Testament, patience means waiting for God for any length of time, not going away, and not giving in to boredom or discouragement. It is the demeanor of the servent in the Gospel who waits even though his master is delayed his return until after midnight. Patience is the supreme quality of the Inner ife and of unconditional love. This charismatic dimension must be the basis of minstry in the twenty-first century.`

9

Priestly Spiritual Formation with Centering Prayer

SANDRA CASEY-MARTUS

Halfway through the spring semester of my final year of seminary training, I had had enough. Naively perhaps, I came to seminary in mid-life to find a deeper life of prayer, spiritual guidance, and community. Instead, I encountered an intellectual "boot camp." I thought I would have to leave the academy, find a "real" job, and get my hands dirty again out in the fields of the Lord (*if* I could find a vineyard). I was frustrated with the lack of balance in seminary, and my prayer life had not progressed as I had hoped when I began. It all came to a head in an ethics class.

The lecture topic was divine retribution, the consequences of and punishment for sin. Personally, I was more interested in divine *union* with God and *freedom* from the consequences of sin. The professor drew a hard line with the hackneyed phrase: "You play, you pay." Perhaps because of my own experience of sin, conversion, and reconciliation, or perhaps because of my utter frustration at hearing another matter-of-fact academic rendering of the gospel, up went my hand for permission to speak: "That is not my understanding of the way Jesus dealt with sinners; he responded to those caught 'in the act' in a way they didn't deserve—with unconditional love, mercy, and compassion." I knew one thing for certain in my homestretch to ordination: if any of us were held up to the "you play and you pay" standard, no one (least of all myself) would pass muster. My comment set off a firestorm in the class. I guess I was spoiling for a fight of some sort, but I could have cared less about grades by that point.

In the back of the classroom sat a visitor, an older man, who apparently had enjoyed every word of this heated exchange, although I did not know he was there until later. A classmate told me he had asked my name.

After class the visitor introduced himself to me as John Thornton, the bishop of Idaho. Looking me directly in the eyes, he asked, "So Sandy, just exactly what is your thing?" Without hesitation I spoke in equal candor, "Well, bishop, you probably won't believe me since you've seen that I'm an outspoken extrovert, but if you really want to know what my 'thing' is, it's Centering Prayer, spiritual direction, and teaching theology."

That was the overture to a job offer that would lead me to establish a retreat center and to teach Centering Prayer in an experimental seminary course, perhaps one of the first of its kind, on spiritual formation in the contemplative dimension of the gospel. I did not realize as I went through my own seminary experience earlier that my frustrations had been on-the-job training.

From the beginning I had been seeking a deeper prayer life. Like many students I came to seminary with a varied job and life experience. I was excited to be at a place where I could devote myself to deepening my personal relationship with God. Seminary would be hard work, and yet I hoped it would also strengthen my practice of Centering Prayer by learning other prayer modalities and living in community with those who shared my interests in spirituality. I would come to discover that seminary is a place full of strange surprises.

I remember being elated when I read the mission statement of the seminary as printed in the course catalog:

> The curriculum of the Seminary of the Southwest consists of all that we do on a regular basis in *the preparation of persons of prayer*

> for leadership in the church. The course of common endeavor includes worship, academic study and the practice of ministry. Thus conceived, our curriculum is both innovative and traditional. In its concern for matters of formation and its provision of a core curriculum it is traditional. It is innovative in its structures for *the integration of theory and practice, theological knowledge and personal experience.*[1] [My emphases.]

I already considered myself a "person of prayer." I had over twenty years of experience with meditation beginning with Eastern methods of transcendental meditation. Later I discovered the Christian method of Centering Prayer. I regularly attended an annual eight-day silent retreat and had received fourteen years of guided spiritual direction. I also fancied myself a person of "theological knowledge and personal experience" since I had completed most of my formal seminary training at a Roman Catholic seminary, and had taught theology for five years. With my gender no longer a barrier to the priesthood, I was eager to finish my seminary education with electives in spirituality, prayer, and Anglican studies.

As I read more in the catalog, however, I discovered that the mission statement's emphasis on prayer was not reflected in the course offerings. In the three-year curriculum, there were no course listings on spiritual formation, prayer, or spiritual direction. Instead, I had to settle for a course on the Spanish mystics and every course in pastoral theology that I could schedule, but my disappointment turned into disillusionment.

Clearly, my prayer life would receive no stimulus from the academic side of seminary. I would have to depend on my regular practice of Centering Prayer and to continue with my spiritual director by e-mail or phone. During this time, however, there was a fundamental challenge welling up: Was my spiritual formation for the priesthood not so important as my intellectual formation? I knew spiritual growth generally did not occur through divine intervention or by accident. One had to work at it. Where,

1. *The 1993–94 Catalog of the Seminary of the Southwest,* Austin, Texas, 15.

as a "person of prayer," was my "integration of theory and practice" to be found?

Back in my apartment meditating, I found the noise of dormitory-style living a distraction. Despite the instructions of Centering Prayer that distractions are not supposed to be obstacles—"return ever-so-gently to the sacred word"—I knew I had to find an environment more conducive to prayer. I set out in search of a quiet, sacred place. It did not shock me (much) that there was not a meditation room on campus, but it did surprise me to learn that the chapel was locked both early and late in the day, exactly at the times that most working people pray. A seminary receptionist suggested that if I was interested in finding a quiet place, perhaps I should try the library!

With no alternative I returned to my room, and it was not out of virtue that I followed Jesus's dictum: "Whenever you pray, go into your room and shut the door and pray to your Father who is in secret; and your Father who sees in secret will reward you" (Matt. 6:6). In the privacy of my room I tried to accept the prospect that my spiritual formation for the priesthood—indeed, for my prayer life—would occur primarily in solitude. Of course, many holy people had pursued an active prayer life in less auspicious surroundings; surely I could, too.

The demands of classwork and outside activities threatened to shorten the time I could spend in prayer and meditation. When I complained about this to another student, I was told, "If you want spiritual guidance or formation, you have to find it yourself or go somewhere else. The seminary is for academics." Silent retreats were neither part of the curriculum nor available through the seminary. Only one day each semester was designated a "quiet day," consisting of a full day and evening of chapel lectures, but most students used "quiet day" to catch up on their studying.

Most disappointing, perhaps, was the one occasion in class when *lectio divina* came up as a lecture topic. I was excited at the prospect of hearing more about the ancient monastic practice; I knew that the roots of Centering Prayer lay in that tradition. The professor, however, only discussed the first three steps: *lectio, meditatio,* and *oratio.* He actually knew nothing of *contemplatio,* the final goal of *lectio divina.* Then I recalled Thomas Keating's discussions on this tragic loss of the contemplative dimension of the gospel:

> In the way that history regularly deals with spiritual movements, people tended to get locked into categories. With the tendency to analyze that was so characteristic of the late Scholastic Middle Ages, the spontaneity of the spiritual journey got lost, and the final stage of *lectio,* resting in God—the purpose of all the other stages—tended to be left out. One was expected to do spiritual reading and discursive mediation for X number of years; if one lived to be very old—or maybe on one's deathbed—one might hope for an experience of contemplation. . . . The integral link between *lectio* and contemplation was broken.[2]

I now had a firsthand experience of the continuing reality of this "break." My highly respected professor had not *lost* the knowledge of such prayer practices; he had never been *taught* anything about it! No wonder we had no meditation room or periods of silent prayer. No wonder there was no emphasis on spiritual direction. The opportunity of a practice and nurture of contemplative prayer to help us to heal and grow in holiness—and to prepare for active ministry—had been lost in today's priestly formation.

> The final nail hammered into the coffin of the traditional teaching was that it would be arrogant to aspire to contemplative prayer. Novices and seminarians were thus presented with a highly truncated view of the spiritual life, one that did not accord with scripture, tradition and the normal experience of growth in prayer.[3]

In conversations with other seminarians I pursued this issue, asking them about the relationship between academics and

---

2. Thomas Keating, *Intimacy with God* (New York Crossroad, 1994), 53–54.

3. Thomas Keating, *Open Mind, Open Heart: The Contemplative Dimension of the Gospel* (Rockport, Mass. Element Books, 1986), 25.

spirituality. Everyone agreed that seminary prepared us intellectually but that little attention was paid to our spiritual lives. If our spiritual lives were neglected, our physical bodies were completely ignored as either temples of the Holy Spirit or as vehicles of consciousness as Eastern traditions emphasize. It did not seem like there was much that students could do. Graduation, ordination, and ministry would have to take precedence over spiritual formation. When we were established in our ministries, we could then turn to the care of our souls.

I accepted this reality, too, but it seemed inconceivable that a seminary student could graduate without being taught anything about the forms and disciplines of prayer—or about methods for teaching *others* to pray! By the end of the first semester, I decided to stop looking and stop complaining. I was grateful that I had an established practice of prayer. I was just going to do it and give it all over to God.

Early in the second semester, however, a staff member approached me with a request. A group of women at her church had a keen interest in Centering Prayer, and she asked if I might be willing to do a Lenten series on Centering Prayer at her parish. Even though I had not received formal training, I agreed. There were no trained teachers in the Austin area, but my eagerness to try may also have been because I hoped to find kindred spirits interested in prayer. I had been so keenly focused on what I would *receive* in seminary—how good an experience I was going to have—that I had lost sight of what I had to *give*. After an adult life of giving to my kids and to service organizations, this was a delectable irony: maybe I was tired of giving, but God had not tired of asking it of me.

The Lenten series at All Saints Church, where I led ten interested parishioners in the practice of Centering Prayer, revived my hopes. The series was well received, and soon seminarians heard about it, asking for my help with the discipline. As I taught my colleagues, I realized that they were as hungry for a deeper form of personal prayer as I was. We all just needed a voice and a method like Centering Prayer for approaching this dimension of prayer.

That was the context for my encounter with Bishop Thornton after my ethics class. I feared the impression he must have received from my outburst. I was reassured and excited, however, when he invited me to lunch and asked me to bring my transcripts. During lunch he was engaging and encouraging. He asked if I would give him permission to contact my own bishop concerning a placement in the Diocese of Idaho. I wanted to say yes but declined, deferring to my bishop's unknown plans for me and confident that whatever happened would be God's will.

My decision to decline gnawed at me, but later in May I was approached with a formal request from Thornton for a six-week summer internship in Wyoming. I got my bishop's permission and accepted. I still did not know what job Thornton wanted me to do—or even where Alta, Wyoming, was on the map—but I was going. I suspected that my future would not be in Texas.

When Bishop Thornton met me at the door of St. Francis of the Tetons, he told me that my job would be to develop a program for the Alta Retreat Center, which did not yet exist, and an educational program for the newly established Mission of St. Francis. I was dumbfounded. This was the realization of a longtime dream to combine retreat work and Christian education—and to devote myself to prayer and spiritual direction. My responsibilities included being lay vicar *and housekeeper.* The bishop would return in six weeks at the end of my internship to see what I had accomplished.

The opportunity to develop a retreat center from the ground up is a great gift—and a daunting task, especially to do so in only six weeks. Except for the bishop, I did not know a soul in Wyoming, so I turned to my logical constituency: I called the dean of students back at the seminary. I asked the dean about the possibility of adding a course titled "The Art and Practice of Christian Prayer" to the January curriculum, which would be an introduction to Centering Prayer and a ten-day intensive silent retreat in Wyoming. The dean is a very practical and tactful person. He listened carefully before reminding me of the many roadblocks: approval of the course, budgetary constraints, and (particularly) the competition from other "required" courses—the new course on prayer could only be offered as an elective. The regular faculty might look askance at a course on spiritual growth held at a ski resort and conducted by a recent graduate. He said nothing about the prospects for approval, but he encouraged me to submit a proposal for the course.

Weeks later the dean called back with excitement in his voice. My course had been approved for three elective credits, but there were restrictions: only six students could sign up, a full-time faculty member would monitor the course, the seminary would not provide funding, and there would be no stipend for me. I snapped right back to reality: Was this just a polite way of saying no? How would I fund it? After all, where would I find the airfare of $400 per seminarian, never mind food and retreat fees? I realized, though, that he was giving me a chance, and I remembered the seminary mission statement: "innovative in its structures for the integration of theory and practice, theological knowledge and personal experience." My belief in seminary education, long moldering in the tomb (so to speak), was reviving.

Somehow it all came together after a flurry of grant requests and proposals. We received grants from the Episcopal Church Foundation and the presiding bishop. When no faculty member volunteered to monitor the course, the seminary's provost, Bill Bennett, agreed to be our faculty sponsor and resident priest. It was snowing in the Tetons on the day the seminarians landed in Jackson Hole. I was making the beds and sweeping the retreat center. Having raised two children, I felt the nurturing side of my spirituality moving into broader, priestly dimensions. Standing exactly where Thornton had met me six months earlier, my heart was full of thanksgiving as I watched the participants arrive at the church door for the beginning of the retreat.

Silence is a great equalizer. You achieve intimacy with others so much more effectively than you can with words. A silent retreat with Centering Prayer for eight days cultivates intimacy not only with other participants but with our God who speaks in silence—if we can be quiet and listen attentively.

The shared intention to be open and available to God's action and presence sustained the participants. My own experience was otherwise. During the first two days everyone was falling asleep at every meditation period! Everyone was sleeping at every opportunity. Most had just finished ordination and/or semester exams. After two days of "narcolepsy," one angry participant complained, "I didn't come here to sleep! I came here to meet God." She had staked out a corner of the prayer room and built a perimeter around her meditation area with an array of tissues, potions, lotions, and cold pills. Like Buddha under the banyan tree, she had come for *results,* but she just kept nodding off—until a certain humility asserted itself in her helpless fight against sleep.

Eventually, Bill Bennett remarked, "I just can't believe how tired the students are and how much they can sleep." I was fearful that he would report negatively about the January "ski vacation," but I knew what was happening. Keating's concept of "Divine Therapy" was at work.[4] In the deep rest that the prayer provides, the body's storehouse of undigested and unprocessed psychological debris is allowed to surface and evacuate. Combining this with end-of-term exhaustion results in the sleepiness, aches, and irritations that happen during the initial stages of retreat. I had anticipated this response by hiring a massage therapist. Simple restorative techniques and relaxation postures were introduced to facilitate the purification process.

I quietly encouraged participants to rely on the program's structure and to trust that it would provide boundaries and safety. With our daily rhythm of Centering Prayer, simple meals, and contemplative Eucharists, the predictability created security and familiarity, allowing everyone to enter more deeply into God's presence. By the fourth day everyone was awake, alert, and responsive. The retreat was beginning to effect God's work.

On the night of the fourth silent day I thought it was time to take the risk of listening to the participants. We gathered in chapel for a liturgy of reconciliation. During the *lectio divina* reflection, people began to talk about their experience so far, commenting on the connections between the retreat and their spiritual lives. Each one found in Centering Prayer an opportunity for a

---

4. Keating, *Intimacy with God,* 79.

new beginning and a new commitment to spiritual growth within their seminary education and pastoral work. For most, if not all, the retreat was becoming a conversion experience and celebration.

After conversation we dissolved into the music of a soft chant of Taizé, interrupted only by quiet proclamations of absolution, forgiveness, and reconciliation. The retreat only deepened from here. The silence became sacramental as it facilitated everyone's ability to open to deeper and deeper levels of God's presence within us and among us.

The participants' final evaluations underscored the transformative experience that everyone had. All had regained a sense of the centrality of spiritual life. In Centering Prayer many had found a method for further development of that spiritual life. Comments ranged from outright praise for Centering Prayer to a renewed appreciation for liturgy and the Eucharist as a direct result of our silence together with God. Others spoke about the spiritual emptiness of their academic lives so far, and vowed to continue building upon the techniques they had learned. Best of all, though, everyone who "slept" through the January course received three full credit hours!

In spite of the affirmation the course received, both in conversations with participants and in their written evaluations, the true test of its effectiveness lay in the future lives and ministries of the participants. Many questions and implications for seminary education, however, remained unanswered: If contemplative prayer better empowers the minister to meet the needs of a congregation, should it not be a priority in seminary? Could hours of service in the soup kitchen be complemented by hours of silence in the meditation hall? What would a Master of Divinity degree have to include if experiential and theoretical knowledge were given equal weight and time? Do seminarians not need as much care of the body and soul as for the mind?

These questions have powerful and transforming implications for seminary curriculum. Imagine a balanced emphasis on spiritual and intellectual aspects of priestly formation—the integration of physical rest and physical exercise, of private and corporate prayer, of personal reflection and social action—as part of seminary training. These are revolutionary ideas that challenge the traditional notions of theological academia.

Perhaps the significant question is: What will it cost the Church to pay for and encourage spiritual disciplines—or, *at what cost can the Church afford to ignore it?* Many clergy suffer from burnout. There is a deep, spiritual hunger throughout America. If the Church does *not* respond to spiritual needs, people will find answers elsewhere. People want to know *about* God, but more urgently they want to find out *how* to know God.

The Church's rich contemplative tradition can provide not only knowledge of theology but also direct knowledge of God's presence through prayer. The priest who receives a strong spiritual formation can make a difference. If well-versed in the contemplative tradition of Christianity, the priest can offer people the transforming possibility of divine union. In order to be a guide and companion on this spiritual journey, however, one must be familiar with knowledge *and* with spiritual knowing. Ministers must be informed and formed physically, psychologically, intellectually, and spiritually. There must be balance.

Contemplative prayer, opportunities for spiritual guidance, and extended periods of silence are essential as one responds to God's invitation to holiness. There is no substitute or shortcut to the awareness of God's presence. To know God in silence, we must set aside the time on a regular basis for the prayer of adoration, "with or without words."[5] It is this prayer of silent adoration that leads to the *apatheia,* the Christian enlightenment that Evagrius Ponticus wrote about in *Praktikos,*[6] which leads to *agape,* the unconditional love that Jesus made his first and highest commandment. Without this love of Christ's presence and action within us, nurtured in contemplative prayer, we as priests and ministers are just a "noisy gong or clanging cymbal" (1 Cor. 13:1).

---

5. Regarding "Prayer and Worship," see *The Book of Common Prayer* (New York Church Hymnal Corp., 1979), 856.

6. Evagrius Ponticus, *The Praktikos: Chapters on Prayer*, trans. John Eudes Bamberger (Spencer, Mass. Cistercian Publications, 1970), 27–39.

For all of us, the fruits of Centering Prayer (in preparation for the gifts of contemplative prayer) are best expressed by Thomas Keating in his introduction to *Open Mind, Open Heart*:

> Today the Christian churches find themselves with a marvelous opportunity. Many sincere believers are eager to experience contemplative prayer. Along with this aspiration, there is a growing expectation that the leaders of local communities be able to teach the Gospel out of personal experience of contemplative prayer. This could happen if the training of future priests and ministers places formation in prayer and spirituality on an equal footing with academic training. It could also happen if spiritual teaching becomes a regular part of the lay ministry. In any case, until spiritual leadership becomes a reality in Christian circles, many will continue to look to other religious traditions for the spiritual experience they are not finding in their own churches. If there were a widespread renewal of the preaching and practice of the contemplative dimension of the Gospel, the reunion of the Christian churches would become a real possibility, dialogue with the other world religions would have a firm basis in spiritual experience, and the religions of the world would bear a clearer witness to the human values they hold in common.[7]

7. Keating, *Open Mind, Open Heart*, 3.

10

From Conversion to Contemplation: Reflections on a Spiritual Journey

JIM CLARK

There I was: nineteen years old, a red-necked hedonist with a Coors in one hand, a spittoon in the other, and my face buried in a $4.99 drugstore copy of the New Testament. Every word leaped off the page as if God were speaking directly to me. I highlighted and underlined and connected verses, scribbling notes all over the margins. This was the most captivating book I had ever read.

This enthralling encounter with the New Testament actually began several weeks earlier after I had a classic out-of-body experience. One evening while visiting with friends at Oklahoma University, I was suddenly looking down at myself. The experience was not really frightening but welcoming. When it subsided, it left me with two thoughts: that God existed (something I had never before taken seriously) and that I needed to embark upon an urgent search to find "God," even though I did not know who or what God was.

My first impulse was to find a Bible. With only a Sunday School acquaintance of Scripture to orient me, I read randomly at first. Then I started devouring book after book, captivated by the story but still seeking an "interior" meaning for my own experience. One night I happened to stumble across the first eight chapters in the book of Romans. I was spellbound at how Paul's writing expressed the way I had lived: trapped in an alienated, guilt-ridden existence with no way out and no clear direction or meaning. Intellectually, I *understood* for the first time that Jesus' message had a significance and relevance to my life, but I still did not *believe* it—and I certainly did not *believe* in Jesus. I spent most of the night reading Romans. Grateful, exhausted, but still reluctant, I went to sleep.

In the silence of sleep my fear-ridden senses were stilled.[1] Somehow, I awoke the next morning with a huge smile. Without the slightest hesitation or embarrassment, I stood up in bed, raised my hands, and said, "It's Jesus. Jesus is God. Jesus is the way." *How* I knew, I could not say, but the reluctant "yes" of *understanding* that reverberated while reading Romans had, thanks to the silence of sleep, emerged from the core of my being as the "yes" of *believing.*

Fueled by my new discovery that Jesus was real and that he had made himself known to me, I realized he was now speaking to me through the Scriptures. I could not get enough of the God of the universe who had revealed Himself[2] to me, and I could not get enough of the Scriptures, through which I was now being led to a deeper experience and understanding.

As I shared my experience with skeptical friends and family, they suggested I find an established church community (probably hoping someone else would bring me back to "normalcy"). However, bell towers and steeples were not what I needed. Instead, I found my way to an abandoned airplane hangar housing a charismatic church called The Christian Center. There, the young assistant pastor immediately identified my unusual spiritual awakening

1. See stanza 7 of "Dark Night," *The Poems of John of the Cross,* trans. Willis Barnstone (Bloomington: Indiana University Press, 1968), 41.

2. The masculine is used here for convenience but with full reverence to the Wisdom tradition, the feminine aspect of God.

as a conversion. I was amazed at his ability to elucidate my spiritual experience with scriptural references, to make me feel that my experiences were normal. I stayed all afternoon talking, and with evening approaching he invited me to join him in the "prayer closet," a small, dark room (so named after Jesus's instructions in Matt. 6:6). The assistant pastor knelt in front of a folding chair, put his elbows on the seat, and buried his face in his hands. Suddenly he began shouting, "Jesus! Jesus! Oh precious *Jesus!*" I nearly jumped out of my skin! All that kept me from bolting out the door was that this devout stranger had seen Christ in my experience, whereas family and friends had suspected instability, drug abuse, or delusion.

Undaunted, I attended services that Sunday in the large hangar. There were ecstatic utterances, prophecies prefaced by "Thus says the Lord," and an utterly alien language, *glossolalia* ("speaking in tongues"). It was strange and uncomfortable, but again I stayed because these "gifts of the Spirit" were resonating with my own growing prayer experiences.

I have come to think of those first few weeks of being captivated by the Christian faith—rapturous experiences of wonder, excitement, gratitude, praise, and simple adoration—as the moment of my conversion. I did not have the slightest notion that concentrated—indeed, deeply packed[3]—in these first experiences were my next twenty-five years of growth through grace and formation through Scripture: fundamentalist Bible instruction, para-church inductive Bible studies, a B.A. in New Testament studies, a regular practice of devotional Greek, an M.Div. with an emphasis in New Testament, Holy Orders in the Episcopal Church, and the discovery of *lectio divina* as a context for my continuing growth into interior silence, the contemplative dimension of the gospel.

---

3. From the Book of Acts through the letters of Paul, the story of Paul's conversion on the road to Damascus has an expansive quality, as if over the years Paul gained greater clarity and fuller understanding of his conversion. However, the seeds of all that he would come to understand and do were in that original encounter of his conversion and calling.

I see now that in my conversion were already the seeds of three different perspectives on Christian prayer and spirituality: evangelical, charismatic, and contemplative. From the evangelical dimension there was an enlightened understanding of Scripture leading to faith and transformation. The charismatic experience of being filled with the Holy Spirit empowered me with gifts to live and share the gospel. Finally, there was the contemplative dimension of the gospel, the interior silence of God's living presence through which faith and love are ultimately purified. I have come to see these three perspectives as profoundly complementary in my search for God.

The Evangelical Dimension

FAITH WAS THUS born in me in a typical evangelical fashion: through the proclamation of the gospel or, as Paul explains, "faith comes from what is heard, and what is heard comes through the word of Christ" (Rom. 10:17). This initial encounter with grace through the Scriptures led to the practice of prayerfully reflecting upon the sacred writings. Completely unaware of the "battle for the Bible" or the many "quests for the historical Jesus," I saw the Scriptures had the ability to speak to my own life, which convinced me of their inspiration and authority. Even after years of theological education, leading me through many layers of biblical criticism, it is those first vibrant experiences of prayer that still convince me of Scripture's power to bring one to faith and transformation.

I soon learned that my call to read and reflect upon the Bible was commonly known in evangelical circles as "praying the Scriptures." It is a dynamic process of experiencing the Word as "living and active, and sharper than any two-edged sword, piercing until it divides soul from spirit, joints from marrow; it is able to judge the thoughts and intentions of the heart" (Heb. 4:12). It would be twenty years before I would learn that the evangelical approach to Scripture was the same as the foundation of the Christian contemplative tradition, the mystical theology of the church. As Thomas Keating explains, "The word of God is the source of Christian contemplation. Listening to that word at deepening levels of attention is the traditional method of apprenticeship to contemplative prayer."[4] This method of listening to the word "at deepening levels of attention" came to be referred to as *lectio divina,* "divine reading."

The Charismatic Dimension

THE PRACTICE OF prayer and reflection upon the Scriptures continued to shape me over time. I noticed that my experience of the gifts of the Spirit grew both privately and publicly, and that these gifts became more integrated in my personality and behavior. The healing power of the gospel affected me more deeply. As the seasons passed, the light of Scripture and the Holy Spirit exposed new layers of fear and inadequacy.

As prayer deepened, I experienced healing at many levels. There still remained, however, an interior brokenness that resisted God's love. Over and over in prayer Jesus had spoken to me of his accepting love and mercy, of his calling and place for me. I had experienced "deliverance" and "healing of memories"—and had ministered in these gifts—and yet nothing seemed to help me. There remained a stubborn compulsion that refused to go away. I was driven to perform, excel, and overachieve, almost always at the expense of family. Much of my life betrayed the trust in the gospel I espoused. As many priests will acknowledge, ordination only heightened the need to perform and achieve.

There were always more people to whom I needed to prove my worth and more work to do in the service of God. Slowly, I began to realize the only master I could not please was myself. I was living a contradiction. On the one hand, I had a rich prayer life; on the other, my life of prayer was still not addressing my deepest insecurities.

It was not entirely like that. There were still powerful experiences in prayer that recalled the deep connection of conversion. These moments heightened my sense of reconciliation and

---

4. Thomas Keating, *Intimacy with God* (New York: Crossroad, 1994), 146.

intimacy with God, and these heights of prayer contributed to a growing silence in my prayer life. In the first decade of my Christian life, intimacy with God was often expressed through thanksgiving, praise, and adoration, frequently accompanied by charismatic gifts. In the second decade I experienced a growing intimacy that left me quiet and still.

A Growing Silence

THE TRANSITION FROM the active dimensions of prayer (discursive and affective) to the receptive mode of "resting in God" was hardly as dramatic as the beginning of my spiritual journey. At times moments of exuberance would leave me speechless and wanting merely to be still, but I did not know how to remain in that still place. At other times there was a pervasive and insistent dryness in prayer, sometimes lasting for months. Between these extremes I seemed to be hitting a wall. The fullness of prayer had abandoned me, and yet I knew that something more awaited me, that something was drawing me toward it. I now see that I was beginning to move beyond the *effects* of God's presence—beyond insights, beyond the purification of desert experiences, beyond the gifts of the Spirit and responses of prayer and praise—to a more immediate experience of God in pure silence and free of thoughts.

This was a development that I did not expect. My evangelical instruction and teaching about prayer emphasized the *active* dimension: vigorous study and meditation on Scripture, intercessions, thanksgiving, confession, praise, and so on. I can recall no prayer instruction on how to remain silent and listen to God, or how to cultivate silence in prayer. However, there were many references to silent prayer circulating in evangelical circles, particularly in scriptural quotations, such as, "For God alone my soul waits in silence; from him comes my salvation" (Ps. 62:1). Perhaps my need "to perform" caused me to read such passages as instructions to pull back from a busy, active life and spend more time alone in the "activity" of prayer. I did not hear in the Scripture a call to the silent, receptive, contemplative dimension of the gospel even though I was increasingly moving from active, discursive prayer, including the charismatic gifts of the Spirit, to the stillness of quiet adoration. It was not until I was exposed to the Christian contemplative tradition, the mystical theology of the church, that I would enter more fully into the gift of contemplative prayer.

Centering Prayer and the Contemplative Dimension of the Gospel

I DISCOVERED THE contemplative dimension of the gospel while on a retreat. The director suggested reading Thomas Keating's *Open Mind, Open Heart.* His description of the spiritual life in the Christian contemplative tradition was almost completely new to me. As I read Keating's work, I realized that this tradition was speaking of the same journey that I began twenty years before in an evangelical context. Unsettled, I heard the Protestant in me asking, "Can anything good come from the Roman Catholic tradition?"

Perhaps it was this description by Keating that hooked me:

> Contemplative prayer is a process of interior transformation, a conversation initiated by God and leading, if we consent, to divine union. One's way of seeing reality changes in this process. A restructuring of consciousness takes place which empowers one to perceive, relate and respond with increasing sensitivity to the divine presence in, through, and beyond everything that exists.[5]

Throughout Keating's volume I recognized many conceptual similarities to evangelical Protestantism that were expressed in different terms. What Keating refers to as a "restructuring of consciousness" I had learned as the transformation brought about by reflecting upon and attempting to "live the Scripture in the power of the Holy Spirit." I realized that Keating's concepts of "Transforming Union and Divine Union" were what I had learned to express as "abiding in Christ."[6]

---

5. Thomas Keating, *Open Mind, Open Heart: The Contemplative Dimension of the Gospel* (New York: Amity House, 1986), 4.

6. Thomas Keating, *Invitation to Love: The Way of Christian Contemplation* (New York: Continuum, 1996), 101–3.

My encounter with Keating's work went beyond discovering a similar conceptual framework expressed in different semantics. I found my own evangelical and charismatic understanding of these truths deeply enriched by looking at them from contemplative perspectives. It helped me immensely, for example, to think of "being led by the Spirit" (or as Jesus described it, "I only do what I see the Father doing") as Keating's concept of perceiving "all things in God and God in all things."[7] Keating's language emphasizes the intimate experience of unity with God while continuing to recognize God as the Other. Also, Keating's facility in applying contemporary psychological terms to spiritual concepts helped my consciousness see more easily these truths in everyday life.

However, the most dramatic complementary nature between the evangelical and contemplative traditions was the fundamental emphasis on Scripture, in the practice of *lectio divina,* and what I had come to refer to as transformational Bible study, or "praying the Scriptures." In reading Keating I began to suspect that *lectio divina's* fourth sense of Scripture, *contemplatio* ("resting in God"), was what had been drawing me like a moth to the flame. Keating's revitalization of this ancient tradition allowed me to recognize "resting in God" as not only instinctive but perhaps the very dimension that was trying to come to fruition in my own journey. As I pondered Keating's teaching about the silence of contemplation as the end of the practice of *lectio divina,* my own increasingly frequent experiences of silence in prayer were receiving clarity and a new framework.

I could have tried to learn Centering Prayer from Keating's book, but my conversion and later experience in the fellowship of other, more experienced Christians suggested a different path. I therefore attended an introductory workshop on Centering Prayer sponsored by Contemplative Outreach.[8] There I learned

---

7. Keating, *Invitation to Love*, 102.

8. A lay-based, ecumenical organization committed to the process and transmission of Christian transformation through teaching Centering Prayer and the dynamic process of *lectio divina,* and supporting those who practice it.

the method of Centering Prayer as a means of preparing for contemplative prayer. As I learned and practiced the teaching of the Christian contemplative tradition, I slowly began to understand more clearly what had been happening during my own prayer times, and I was able to enter more fully into the silence of contemplative prayer.

After continued practice with Centering Prayer, I also found that the compulsiveness that had proven so resistant was beginning to recede. I do not mean to imply that Centering Prayer became a "cure-all"—quite the contrary. The practice was deepening my relationship of intimacy with Christ, which was resulting in deeper healing, but this was not an altogether new dimension of relationship. Rather, it was bringing to completion what God had given birth to in me twenty years before, and what had been nurtured in the evangelical and charismatic practice of prayer and spirituality. As the gift of God's presence was deepening and maturing, the anxieties and obsessions that fueled my need to perform, to please, and to prove myself were being healed.

The yearning for silence and solitude in the presence of God had been growing in me for years. Contemplative prayer was the end of that yearning; it added a deep sense of completion to my prayer life and relationship with Christ. Not, of course, that I was seeing the end of the spiritual journey at hand. Rather, I had found the understanding and instruction that made more sense of my experiences in prayer and resulted in greater fulfillment in my calling to prayer and relationship with God.

Toward a Common Ground— Complementary Prayer Traditions

MY MOVEMENT INTO contemplative prayer has not been, at the same time, a movement away from evangelical and charismatic prayer. Contemplative prayer has, rather, served to mature and enrich these other dimensions of my spiritual journey. The evangelical tradition's emphasis on the power of Scripture to renew and transform continues to be a vital part of my prayer life. I have not discovered a time in which Scripture is not needed to renew the mind (Rom. 12:3) and to instruct the mind of Christ (1 Cor. 2:16). The joy of discovering and applying the truth of God's Word to my life continues as spiritual food indeed. Moreover, as times of reflecting on the Scripture move me to the silence of contemplation, Centering Prayer allows me to remain in that silence, letting the immediacy of God's presence perform its transforming work. The charismatic gifts of the Spirit also continue to function in my life and ministry, both publicly and privately.

I do not mean to suggest that contemplative prayer is more "spiritual" than evangelical or charismatic spirituality. That would be too simplistic an assessment. Rather, I understand each of them as a necessary dimension of a whole spirituality. My prayer life and ministry continue to be nurtured by the practices I have learned from each of these traditions, and—indeed—each is enriched, informed, and supported by the other.

I believe that in their common search for God, the evangelical, charismatic, and contemplative prayer traditions have great potential to educate and support one another. Certainly, my own spiritual journey has been greatly enriched by drinking from that deep river that flows from the confluence of each of these wellsprings of Christianity.

Appendix ❀

The Method of Centering Prayer

THOMAS KEATING

Theological Background

THE GRACE OF Pentecost affirms that the risen Jesus is among us as the glorified Christ. Christ lives in each of us as the Enlightened One, present everywhere and at the times. He is the living Master who continuously sends the Holy Spirit to dwell within us to bear witness to his resurrection by empowering us to experience and manifest the fruits of the Spirit and the Beatitudes both in prayer and action.

Lectio Divina

Lectio divina is the most traditional way of cultivating friendship with Christ. It is a way of listening to the texts of Scripture as if we were in conversation with Christ and he were suggesting the topics of conversation. The daily encounter with Christ and reflection on his word leads beyond mere aquaintanceship to an attitude of friendship, trust, and love. Conversation simplifies and gives way to communing, or as Gregory the Great (sixth century), summarizing the Christian contemplative tradition, put it, "resting in God." This was the classical meaning of contemplative prayer for the first sixteen cenuries.

Contemplative Prayer

CONTEMPLATIVE PRAYER IS the normal development of the grace of baptism and the regular practice of *lectio divina.* We may think of prayer as thoughts or feelings expressed in words. But this is only one expression. Contemplative prayer is the opening of mind and heart — our whole being — to God, the Ultimate Mystery, beyond thoughts, words, and emotions. We open our awareness to God whom we know by faith is within us, closer than breathing, closer than thinking, closer than choosing — closer than consciousness itself. Contemplative prayer is a process of interior purification leading, if we consent, to divine union.

The Method of Centering Prayer

CENTERING PRAYER IS a method designed to facilitate the development of contemplative prayer by preparing our faculties to cooperate with this gift. It is an attempt to present the teaching of earlier time (e.g., *The Cloud of Unknowing*) in an updated form and to put a certain order and regularity into it. It is not meant to replace other kinds of prayer; it simply puts other kinds of prayer into a new and fuller perspective. During the time of prayer we consent to God's presence and action within. At other times our attention moves outward to discover God's presence everywhere.

The Guidelines

I. Choose a sacred word as the symbol of your intention to consent to God's presence and action within.

II. Sitting comfortably and with eyes closed, settle briefly and silently introduce the sacred word as the symbol of your consent to God's presence and action within.

III. When you become aware of thoughts, return ever-so-gently to the sacred word.

IV. At the end of the prayer period, remain in silence with eyes closed for a couple of minutes.

Explanation of the Guidelines

I. "Choose a sacred word as the symbol of your intention to consent to God's presence and action within." (cf. *Open Mind, Open Heart,* chap.5)

1. The sacred word expresses our intention to be in God's presence and to yield to the divine action.

2. The sacred word should be chosen during a brief period of prayer asking the Holy Spirit to inspire us with one that is especially suitable to us.
   a. Examples: *Lord, Jesus, Father, Mother, Mary;* or in other languages: Kyrie, Jesu, Jeshua, Abba, Mater, Maria.
   b. Other possibilities: *Love, Peace, Mercy, Silence, Stillness, Calm, Faith, Trust, Yes;* or in other languages: *Amor, Shalom, Amen.*

3. Having chosen a sacred word, we do not change it during prayer period, for that would be to start thinking again.

4. A simple inward gaze upon God may be more suitable for some persons than the sacred word. In this case, one consents to God's presence and action by turning inwardly to God as if gazing upon him. The same guidelines apply to the sacred gaze as to the sacred word.

II. "Sitting comfortably and with eyes closed, settle briefly and silently introduce the sacred word as the symbol of your consent to God's presence and action within."

1. By "sitting comfortably" is meant relatively comfortably; not so comfortably that we encourage sleep, but sitting comfortably enough to avoid thinking about the discomfort of our bodies during the time of prayer.

2. Whatever sitting position we choose, we keep the back straight.

3. If we fall asleep, we continue the prayer for a few minutes upon awakening if we can spare the time.

4. Praying in this way after a main meal encourages drowsiness. Better to wait an hour at least before Centering Prayer. Praying in this way just before retiring may disturb one's sleep pattern.

5. We close our eyes to let go of what is going on around and within us.

6. We introduce the sacred word inwardly and as gently as laying a feather on a piece of absorbent cotton.

III. "When you become aware of thoughts, return ever-so-gently to the sacred word."

1. "Thoughts" is an umbrella term for every perception including sense perceptions, feelings, images, memories, reflections, and commentaries.

2. Thoughts are a normal part of Centering Prayer.

3. By "returning ever-so-gently to the sacred word," a minimum of effort is indicated. This is the only activity we initiate during the time of Centering Prayer.

4. During the course of our prayer, the sacred word may become vague or even disappear.

IV. "At the end of the prayer period, remain in silence with eyes closed for a couple of minutes."

1. If this prayer is done in a group, the leader may slowly recite the Our Father during the additional two or three minutes, while the others listen.

2. The additional two or three minutes give the psyche time to readjust to the external senses and enable us to bring the atmosphere of silence into daily life.

Some Practical Points

1. The minimum time for this prayer is twenty minutes. Two periods are recommended each day, one first thing in the morning, and one in the afternoon or early evening.

2. The end of the prayer period can be indicated by a timer, provided it does not have an audible tick or loud sound when it goes off.

3. The principle effects of Centering Prayer are experienced in daily life, not in the period of Centering Prayer itself.

4. Physical symptoms:
   a. We may notice slight pains, itches, or twitches in various parts of our body or a generalized reslessness. These are usually due to the untying of emotional knots in the body.
   b. We may also notice heaviness or lightness in the extremities. This is usually do to a deep level of spiritual attentiveness.
   c. In either case, we pay no attention, or we allow the mind to rest briefly in the sensation, and then return to the sacred word.

5. *Lectio divina* provides the conceptual background for the development of Centering Prayer.

6. A support group praying and sharing together once a week helps maintain one's commitment to the prayer.

Extending the Effects of Centering Prayer into Daily Life

1. Practice two periods of Centering Prayer daily.

2. Read Scriptures regularly and study *Open Mind, Open Heart.*

3. Practice one or two of the specific methods for every day, suggested in *Open Mind, Open Heart,* chap. 12.

4. Join a Centering Prayer support group or follow-up program (if available in your area).
   a. It encourages the members of the group to persevere in private.
   b. It provides an opportunity for further input on a regular basis through tapes, readings, and discussion.

Points for Further Development

1. During the prayer period various kinds of thoughts may be distinguished. (cf. *Open Mind, Open Heart,* chap. 6–10):
   a. Ordinary wanderings of the imagination or memory.
   b. Thoughts that give rise to attractions or aversions.
   c. Insights and psychological breakthroughs.
   d. Self-reflections such as "How am I doing?" or, "This peace is just great!"
   e. Thoughts that arise from the unloading of the unconscious.

2. During this prayer we avoid analyzing our experience, harboring expectations, or aiming at some specific goal such as:
   a. Repeating the sacred word continuously.
   b. Having no thoughts.
   c. Making the mind blank.
   d. Feeling peaceful or consoled.
   e. Achieving a spiritual experience.

3. What Centering Prayer is not:
    a. It is not a technique.
    b. It is not a relaxation exercise.
    c. It is not a form of self-hypnosis.
    d. It is not a charismatic gift.
    e. It is not a para-psychological experience.
    f. It is not limited to the "felt" prescence of God.
    g. It is not discursive meditation or affective prayer.

4. What Centering Prayer is:
    a. It is at the same time a relationship with God and a discipline to foster that relationship.
    b. It is an exercise of faith, hope, and love.
    c. It is a movement beyond conversation with Christ to communion.
    d. It habituates us to the language of God which is silence.

Contributors ❈

SARAH A. BUTLER is canon pastor at St. John's Episcopal Cathedral in Denver, Colorado. She directs the referral service for seniors and trains and coordinates the lay pastoral care program. She gives retreats on spiritual formation and discernment. She is currently writing a ciriculum for training lay pastoral caregivers, emphasizing spiritual reflection and formation as a foundation from ministry. She is a founding member of Christ Centered Ministries, a recognized order of the Episcopal Church.

SANDRA CASEY-MARTUS is vicar of St. Francis of the Tetons Church (Episcopal) and director of the Alta Retreat Center in Wyoming. She was director of campus ministry at Our Lady of the Lake University in San Antonio, and executive director of CONTACT Lubbuck, an ecumenical suicide crisis hotline. She also taught theology at Stone Ridge Country Day School in Bethesda, Maryland. She presently serves on the faculty of Contemplative Outreach, Ltd.

JIM CLARK is associate rector of the Church of Our Saviour Parish (Episcopal) in San Gabriel, California. After graduating from Fuller Theological Seminary, he has spent much of his ministry focusing on spiritual formation and discipleship. He is currently developing a laity-led spiritual formation ministry based on the teaching of Thomas Keating and the practice of Centering Prayer. He serves on the faculty of Contemplative Outreach, Ltd. and has attended numerous retreats and trainings in Centering Prayer.

THOMAS KEATING, OCSO, was born in New York City in 1923. He graduated from Fordham University and entered the Cistercian Order in Valley Falls, Rhode Island, in 1944. He was appointed superior of St. Benedict's Monastery, Snowmass, Colorado, in 1958, and was elected abbot of St. Joseph's Abbey, Spencer, Massachusetts, in 1961. He returned to Snowmass after retiring as abbot of Spencer in 1981, where he established a program of ten-day intensive retreats in the practice of Centering Prayer, a contemporary form of the Christian contemplative tradition. He is one of the architects of the Centering Prayer movement and of Contemplative Outreach, Ltd., an organization that teaches Centering Prayer and provides a support system for those who practice it. He is the author of several books and video/audio tape series. Books currently in print are: *Open Mind, Open Heart; The Mystery of Christ; Invitation to Love; Awakenings; Reawakenings;* and *The Kingdom of God is Like . . .*

PAUL DAVID LAWSON is rector of St. Cross Episcopal Church in Los Angeles. He is currently completing the doctoral program at Claremont School of Theology. He has been a member of the diocesan staff in Los Angeles, a missionary in Saudi Arabia and South America, and a vicar and associate minister. Before ministry he was a political advance person. He is an apprentice balloon pilot, surfer, and former radio DJ. He and his wife Duffy have one son, Boethius. He has practiced and taught Centering Prayer for over twenty years. He serves on the board of trustees of Contemplative Outreach, Ltd.

DAVID WALTON MILLER has been a parish priest for over twenty years, serving at Grace Cathedral in San Francisco, St. James' Wilshire in Los Angeles, and the Church of the Epiphany, San Carlos, California. He is currently rector of the Parish of St. Matthew in Pacific Palisades, California. He was first drawn to the worship of the Taizé while participating in a spiritual director's workshop at Mercy Center, Burlingame, California.

DAVID MORGAN, OCCM, is the canon at large of St. John's Episcopal Cathedral, Denver, Colorado, and the founding prior of the order of Christ Centered Ministries. He served as canon pastor of the St. John's Episcopal Cathedral for fourteen years, and continues this ministry while directing the Contemplative Prayer Outreach Fellowship and its prayer groups. He is a member of the National Faculty and the Board of Trustees of Contemplative Outreach, Ltd. He and his wife Delores have two grown children

THOMAS NEENAN, is director of music at the Parish of St. Matthew (Episcopal), Pacific Palisades, California. He is a lecturer in music history and theory at California Institute of Technology (Caltech) and a member of the executive board of the Anglican Association of Musicians. He is co-founder and conductor of the Chamber Orchestra at St. Matthew's. He has conducted a variety of instrumental and choral ensembles in the United States, Europe, and Japan, and has made several tours of Europe as a recital organist.

M. BASIL PENNINGTON, OCSO, is a monk of St. Joseph's Abbey, Spencer, Massachusetts. Included among his numerous books are *Centering Prayer, Centered Living, Daily We Touch Him, In Peter's Footsteps, Breaking Bread, Challenges in Prayer, The Manual of Life, On Retreat with Thomas Merton,* and *Thomas Merton, Brother Monk.*

GUSTAVE REININGER was instrumental in disseminating Thomas Keating's teaching methods in Centering Prayer beyond the monastic community to those in active life. He is a founder and current trustee of Contemplative Outreach, Ltd. He teaches Centering Prayer and conducts retreats throughout the country. A graduate of the University of Chicago and a former investment banker, he now is a producer, director, and writer of feature films and network television.

THOMAS R. WARD, JR., is chaplain of All Saints' Chapel at the University of the South and teaches in both the college and seminary. He graduated from the College of Arts and Sciences in Sewanee in

1967, Oxford University in England in 1969, and Virginia Theological Seminary in 1975. He has been an active participant and retreat leader at Centering Prayer workshops sponsored by Contemplative Outreach, Ltd. for the last five years. He has worked closely with Thomas Keating, Gus Reininger, and others to offer Centering Prayer more widely, particularly within the Episcopal Church. He serves on the board of trustees of Contemplative Outreach, Ltd.

THOMAS KEATING

CRISIS OF FAITH, CRISIS OF LOVE

Revised and Expanded Edition

"Under the influence of Christian mystics such as St. John of the Cross, Keating weaves a narrative account of spiritual development that will be of . . . interest to spiritual directors and seekers." —*Booklist*

140 pages

WILLIAM A. MENINGER

THE LOVING SEARCH FOR GOD

Contemplative Prayer and The Cloud of Unknowing

"Using the 14th-century spiritual classic *The Cloud of Unknowing* as both a jumping-off place and a sustained point of reference, Meninger, a Trappist monk and retreat master, does a powerful job of explaining contemplative prayer and making it approachable for any seeker. In a nurturing, practical and easy-to-understand manner, and with an obvious affection for his subject, Meninger deals with the yearning search for God through prayer and with the distractions that can impede it—unforgiveness and unforgivenness, will, distortions of imagination, memory, and intellect. The result, filled with humor and built by means of good, solid language that flows beautifully, is an excellent guide for anyone interested in deepening his or her Christian prayer life."

—*Publishers Weekly*

120 pages